Animated PAPER CRAFTS

by Pat Karch

STANDARD PUBLISHING
Cincinnati, Ohio

Library of Congress Catalog Card Number 91-065123

ISBN 0-87403-810-3

Contents

Helpful Hints

Tracing and Transferring a Pattern

1. To transfer a pattern from this book to the paper you are going to use, tape a piece of thin typing paper or tracing paper over the pattern. Trace with a soft-lead pencil. Turn tracing over onto paper to be used and retrace design on back of typing or tracing paper with a hard-lead pencil. By doing it this way your work will be neater, since no pencil marks will show on the right side.

2. If you are going to make several of the same item, glue the paper with the traced design on cardboard and cut out. This pattern can be used again and again by drawing around it.

3. Another way to transfer patterns would be to blacken the back of a traced design with a soft-lead pencil, if you wish to transfer to a light-colored paper. Tape tracing, back side down, to paper you wish to use. Go over the lines of traced design on the right side with a hard-lead pencil. For dark-colored paper use chalk instead of a pencil on the back of tracing paper.

Scoring at Folds

To make cardboard or paper fold easily, run the blade of a pair of scissors or a dull knife lightly along fold line. Hold ruler against line as a guide to assure a straight fold.

Cutting and Gluing

Use a large pair of scissors to cut cardboard and large areas. Use a small pointed pair to cut little things. Rubber cement is best for gluing large areas. White glue is fine for all other parts.

NOAH'S ARK

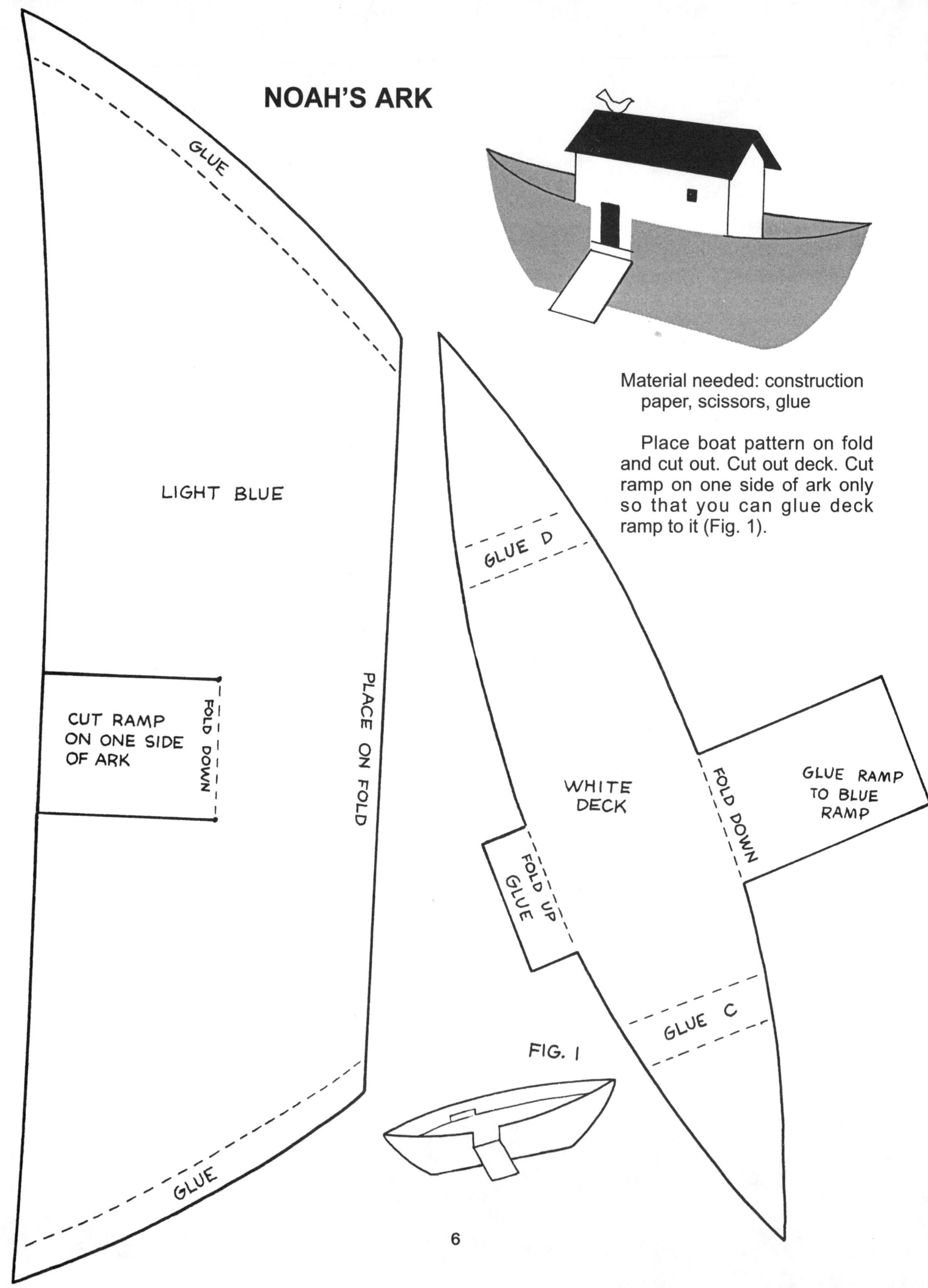

Material needed: construction paper, scissors, glue

Place boat pattern on fold and cut out. Cut out deck. Cut ramp on one side of ark only so that you can glue deck ramp to it (Fig. 1).

6

Cut out and fold cabin. Glue A to A and B to B. Glue onto deck at C and D. Place roof pattern on fold and cut out. Glue on roof (Fig. 2). Cut out dove and insert in slit in roof. Cut out window and glue on. Ramp should form a stand to hold ark upright.

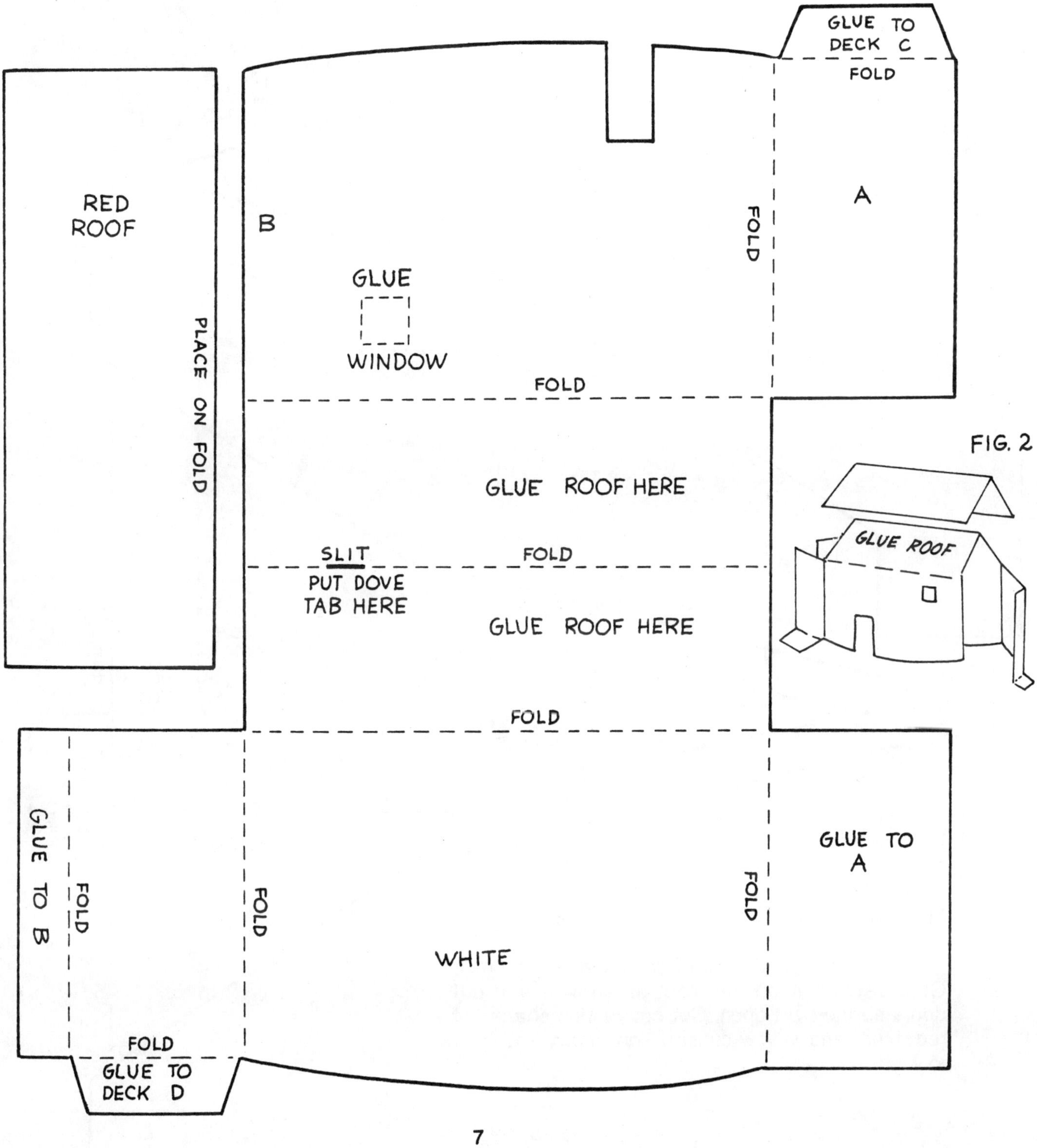

RED ROOF

PLACE ON FOLD

B

GLUE TO DECK C

FOLD

A

FOLD

GLUE WINDOW

FOLD

FIG. 2

GLUE ROOF HERE

SLIT
PUT DOVE TAB HERE

FOLD

GLUE ROOF HERE

FOLD

GLUE TO B

FOLD

FOLD

FOLD

GLUE TO A

FOLD

WHITE

FOLD
GLUE TO DECK D

CHURCH BUILDING

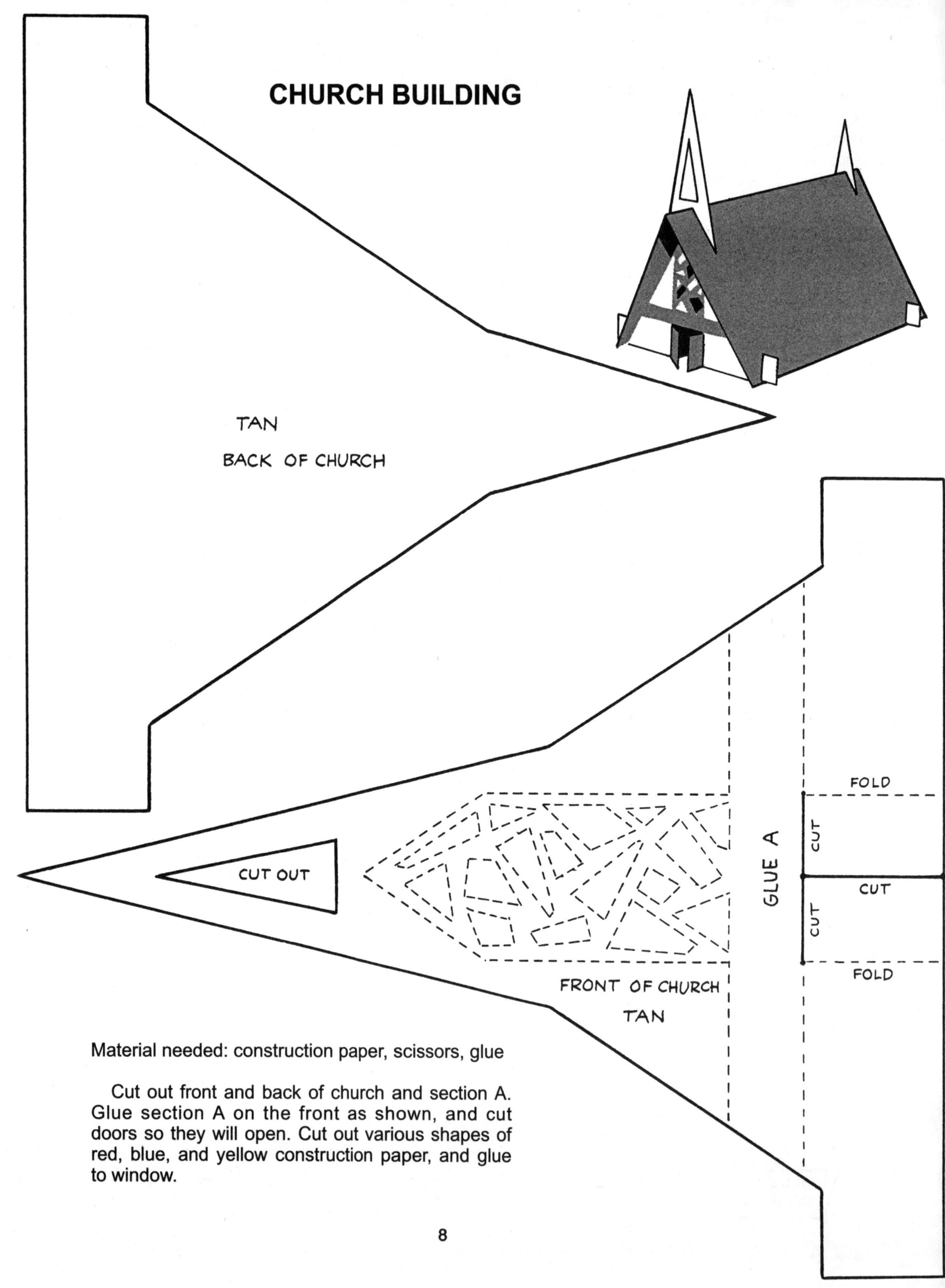

Material needed: construction paper, scissors, glue

Cut out front and back of church and section A.
Glue section A on the front as shown, and cut
doors so they will open. Cut out various shapes of
red, blue, and yellow construction paper, and glue
to window.

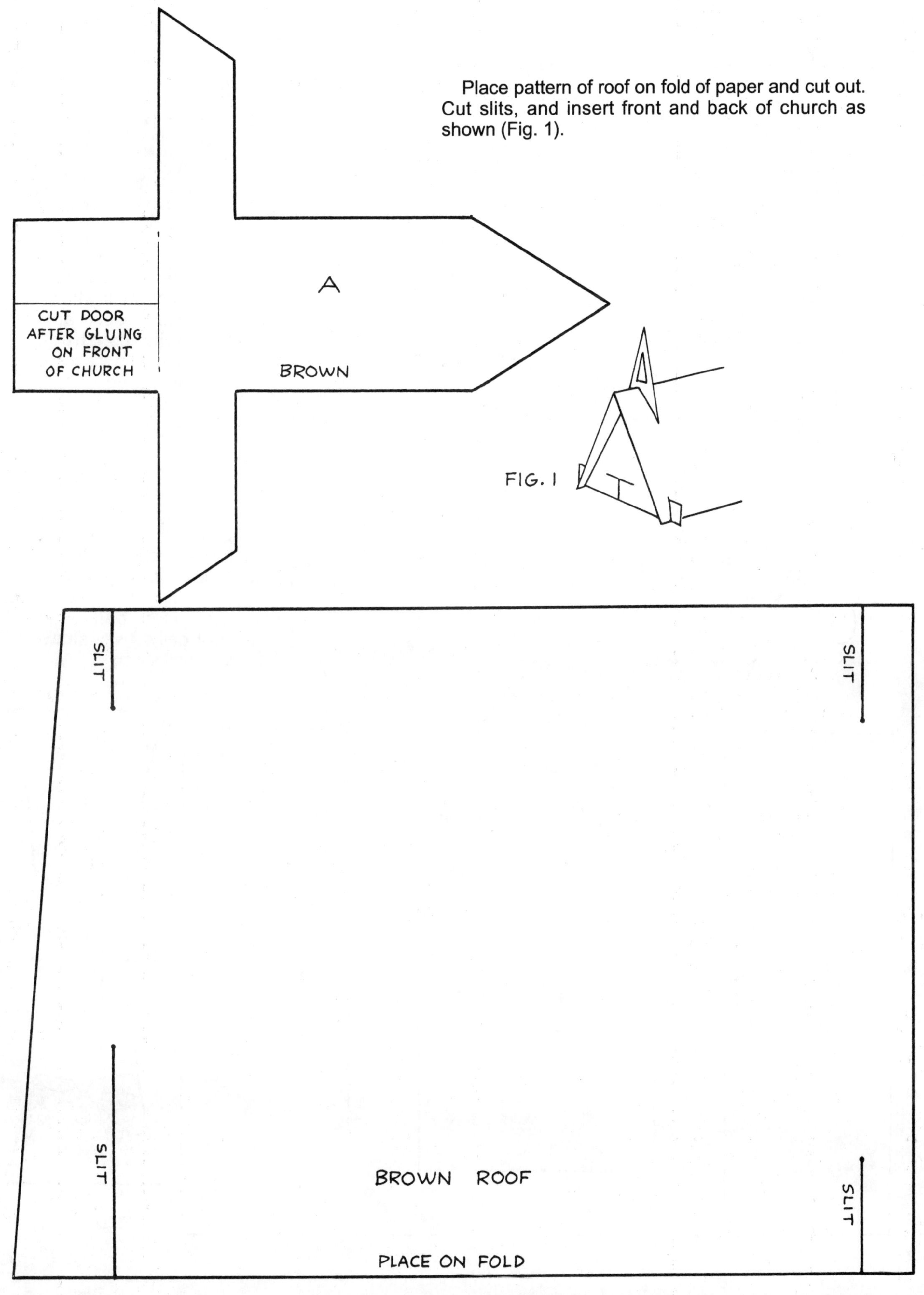

Place pattern of roof on fold of paper and cut out. Cut slits, and insert front and back of church as shown (Fig. 1).
CUT DOOR AFTER GLUING ON FRONT OF CHURCH
A
BROWN
FIG. 1
SLIT
SLIT
SLIT
SLIT
BROWN ROOF
PLACE ON FOLD

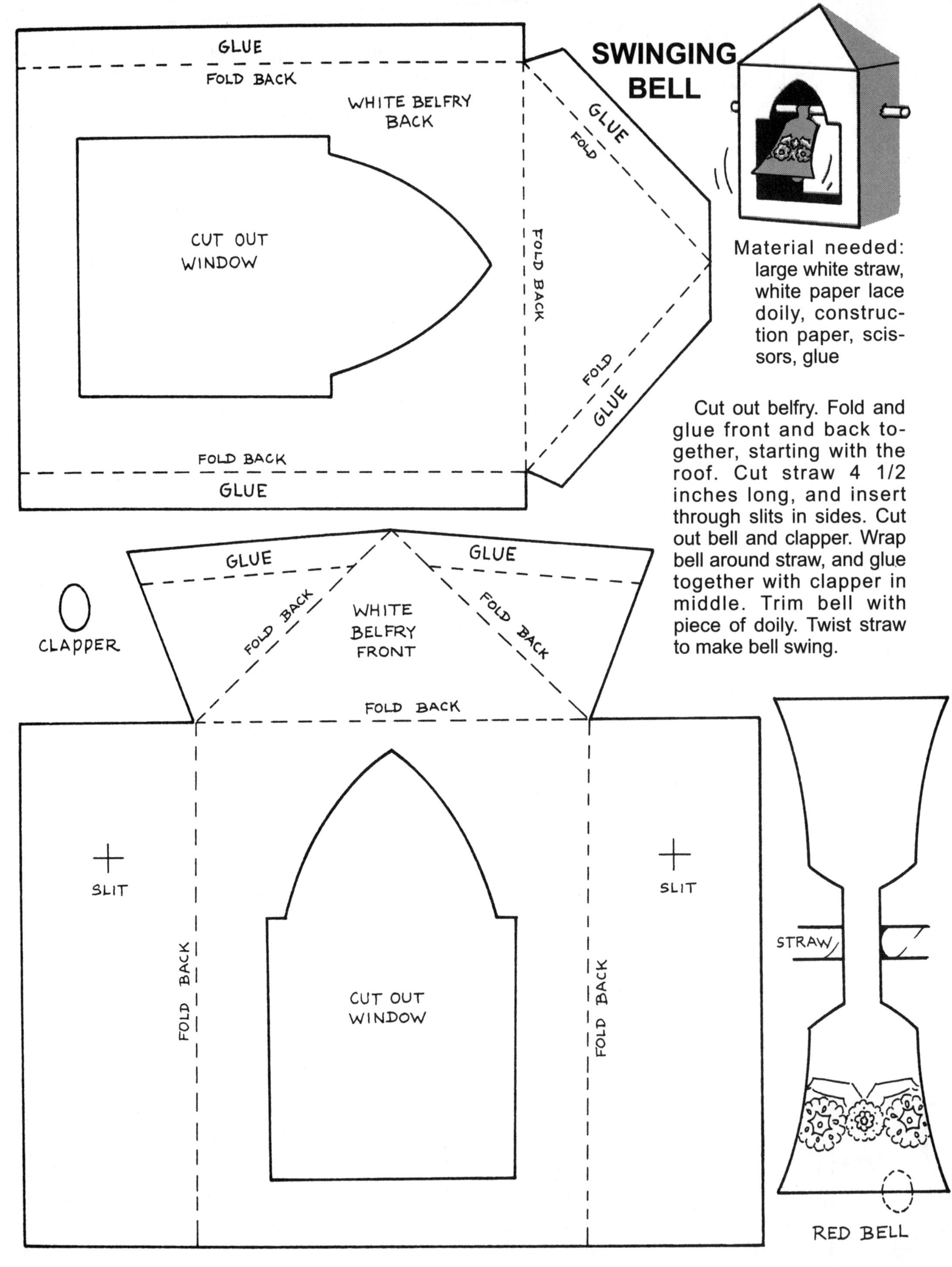

GLUE
FOLD BACK
WHITE BELFRY BACK
CUT OUT WINDOW
GLUE
FOLD
FOLD BACK
FOLD
GLUE
FOLD BACK
GLUE

SWINGING BELL

Material needed: large white straw, white paper lace doily, construction paper, scissors, glue

Cut out belfry. Fold and glue front and back together, starting with the roof. Cut straw 4 1/2 inches long, and insert through slits in sides. Cut out bell and clapper. Wrap bell around straw, and glue together with clapper in middle. Trim bell with piece of doily. Twist straw to make bell swing.

CLAPPER
GLUE
GLUE
FOLD BACK
FOLD BACK
WHITE BELFRY FRONT
FOLD BACK
SLIT
FOLD BACK
CUT OUT WINDOW
FOLD BACK
SLIT

STRAW
RED BELL

JESUS BLESSES THE LITTLE CHILDREN

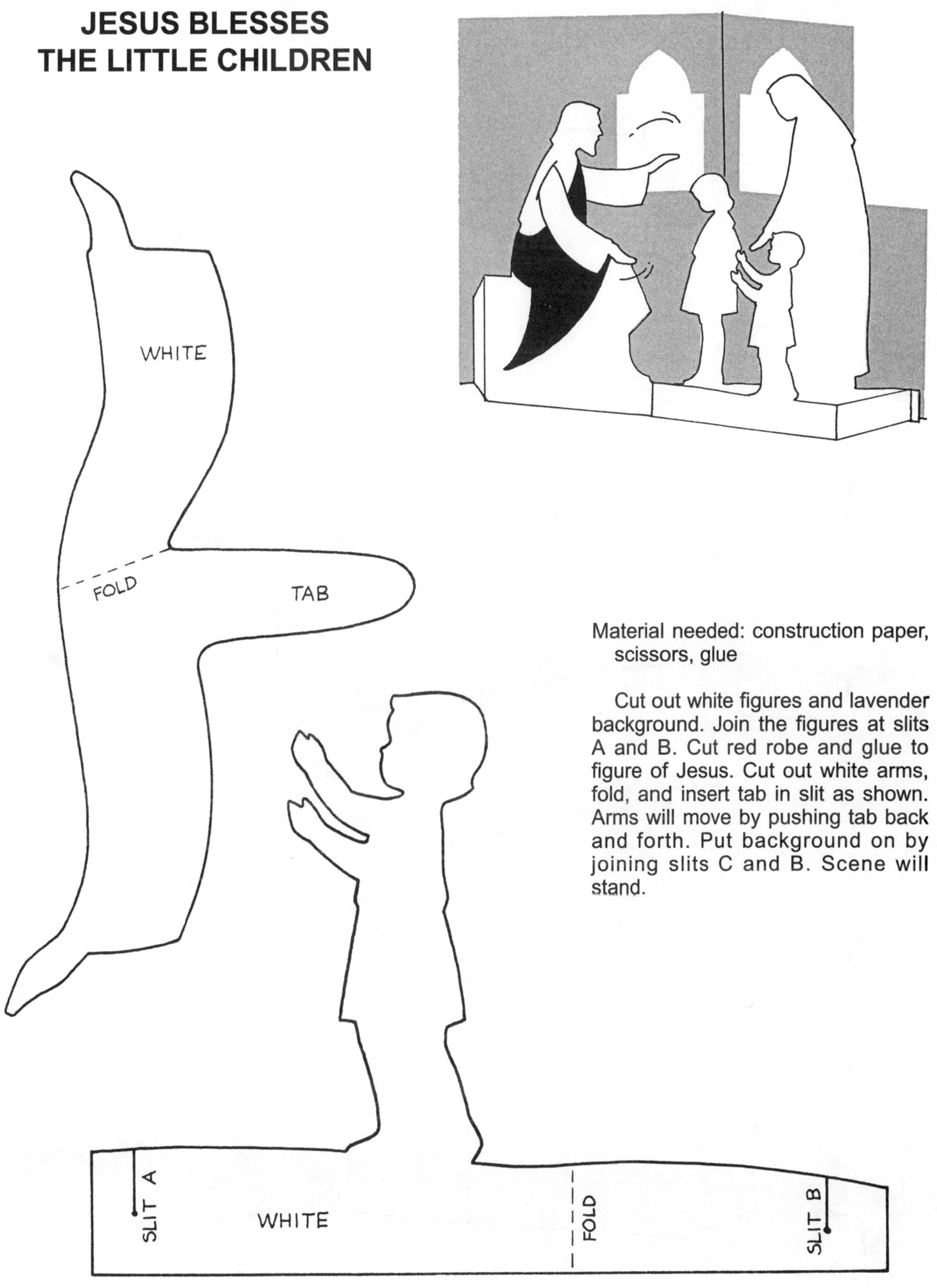

Material needed: construction paper, scissors, glue

Cut out white figures and lavender background. Join the figures at slits A and B. Cut red robe and glue to figure of Jesus. Cut out white arms, fold, and insert tab in slit as shown. Arms will move by pushing tab back and forth. Put background on by joining slits C and B. Scene will stand.

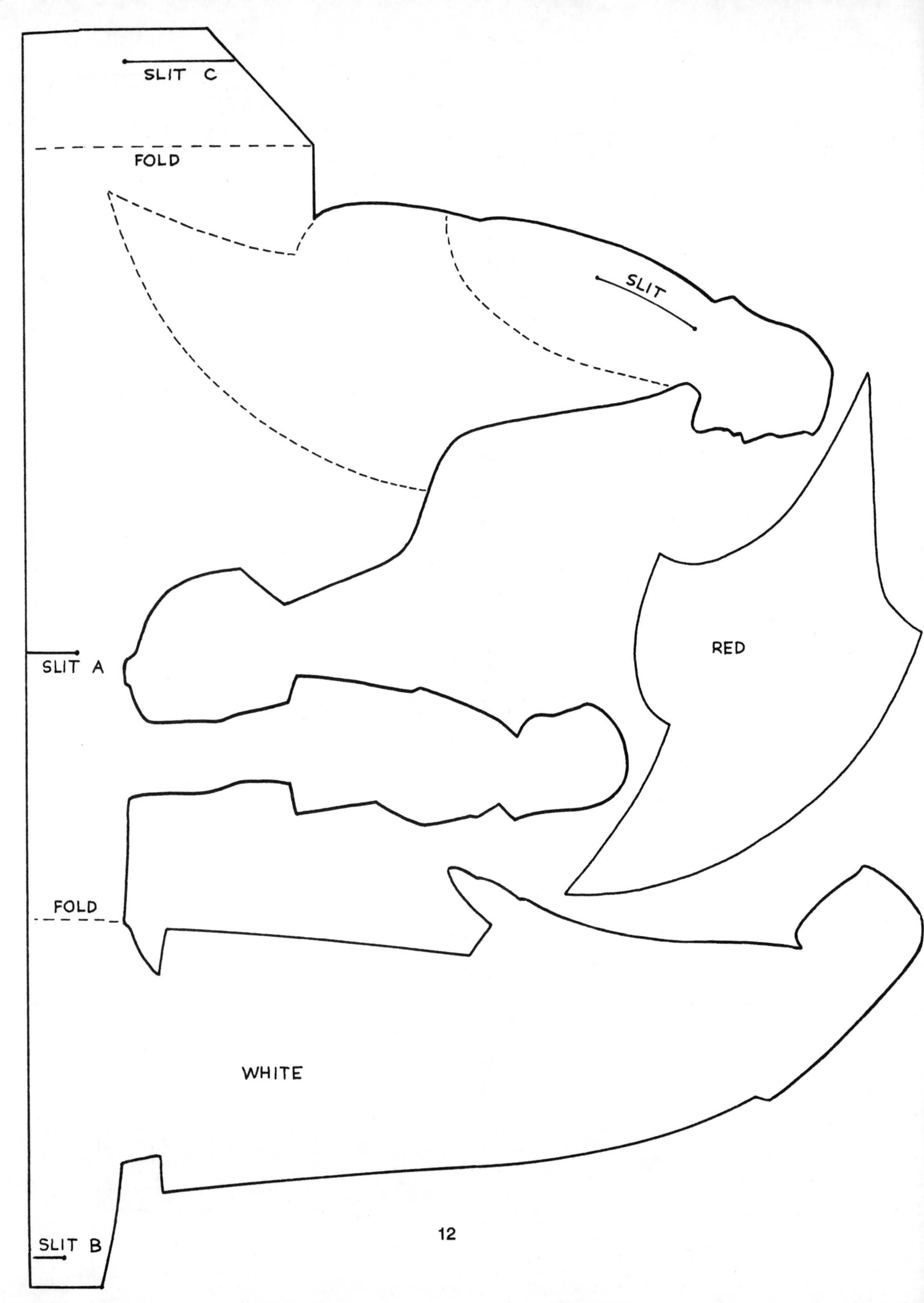

SLIT C
FOLD
SLIT
RED
SLIT A
FOLD
WHITE
SLIT B

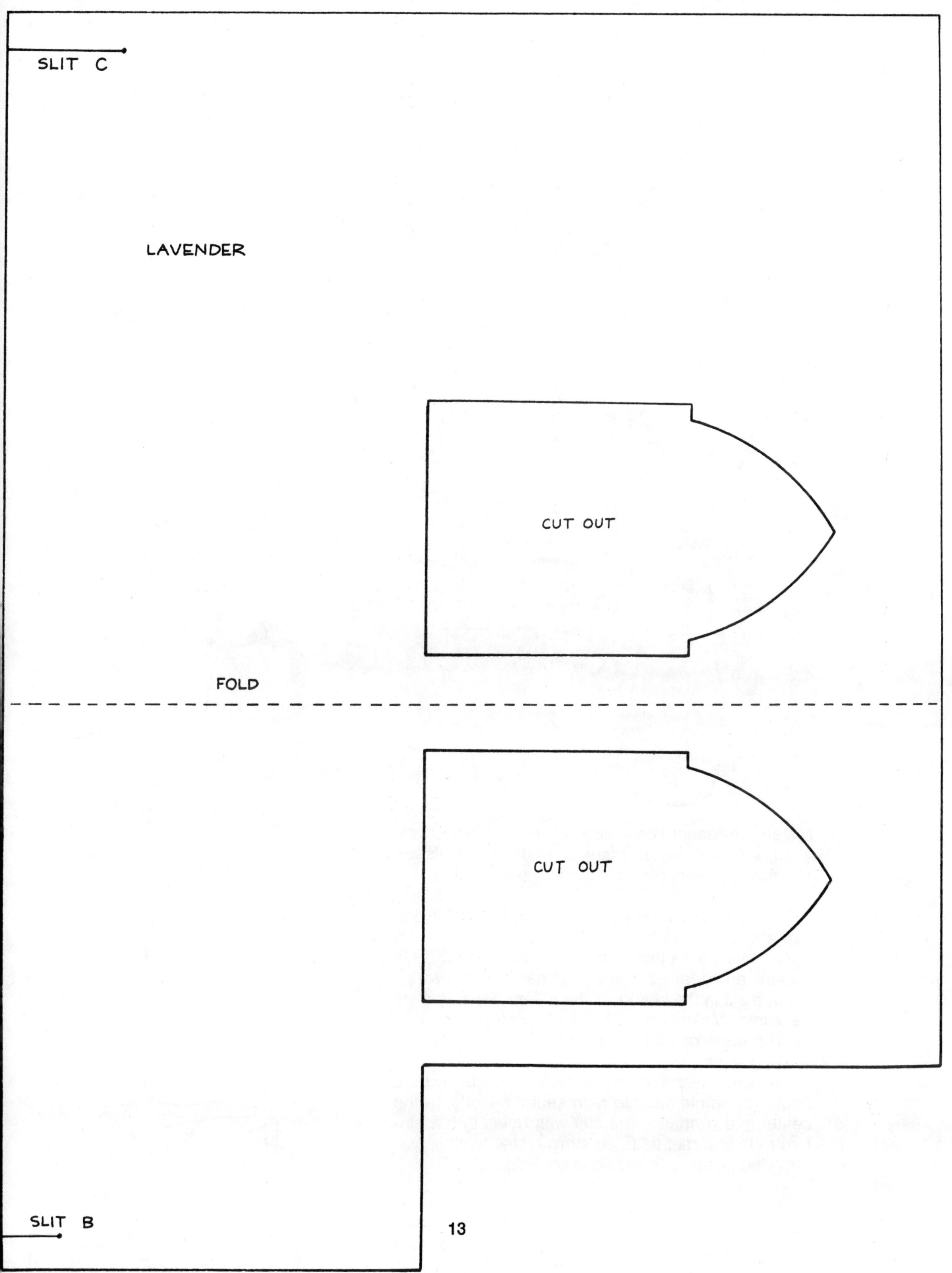

SLIT C
LAVENDER
CUT OUT
FOLD
CUT OUT
SLIT B
13

AROUND THE WORLD CENTERPIECE

Material needed: construction paper, plastic foam cups (3 1/4 inches high) or paper cups, tissue paper, paper or plastic straws, scissors, glue

Two cups are needed for each doll. Cut off one cup about 1 1/2 inches from the bottom to form the base. Invert the other cup and place on top. (This makes an ideal container for candy or favors.) Make a slit in the bottom of the inverted cup to stick neck into. Make slits on sides of cup for arms (Fig. 1). The patterns for the various dolls are on the following pages.

For a centerpiece, cut a 16-inch circle of blue paper (or an old map) to represent the world. In the center, place an inverted cup with holes in the bottom to hold paper flags on straws. Use simple, colorful flag designs as shown in encyclopedias.

"

DUTCH DOLL

Cut out head from white paper. Cut out and glue face and hair. Draw eyes and mouth with a black felt-tip marker. Cut out two arms and stick in side slits of cup, with arms pointed upward. Cut out top and skirt and glue on body cup.

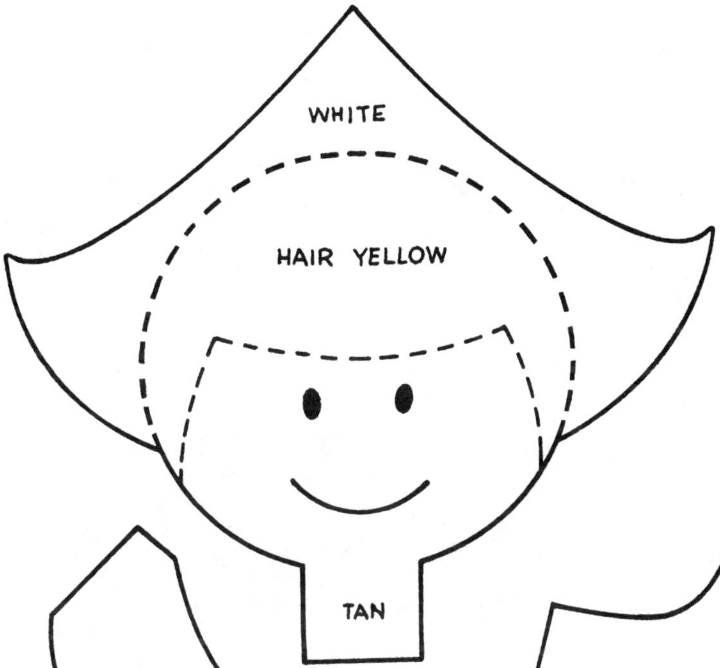

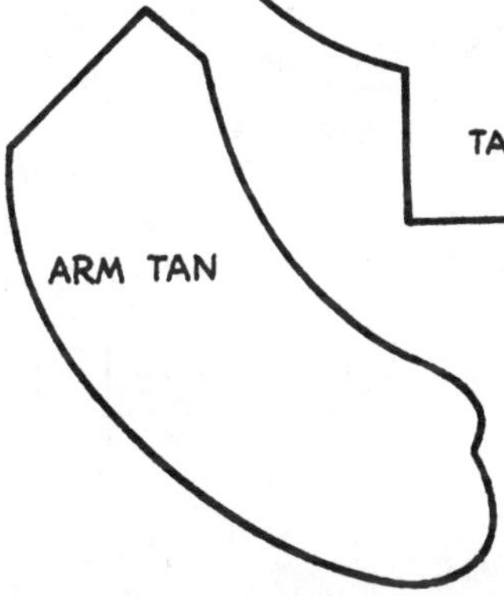

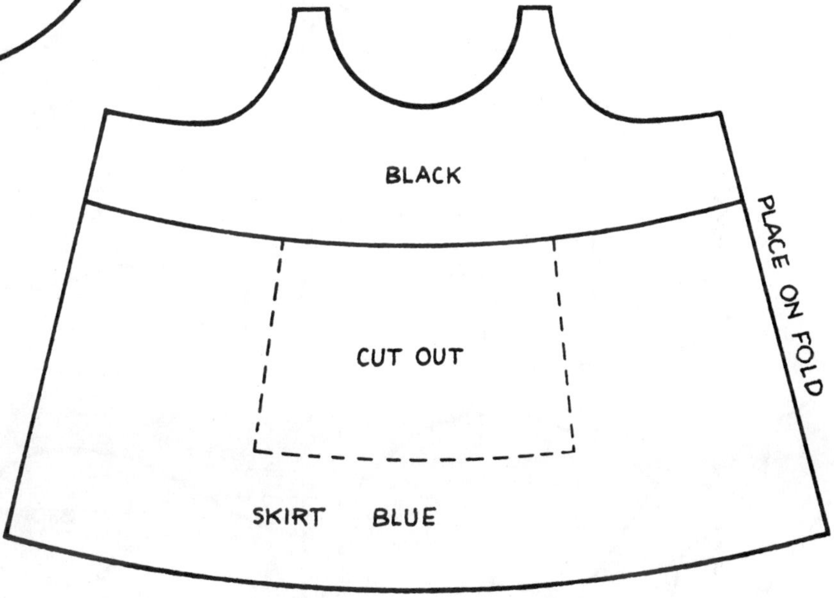

FLAGS

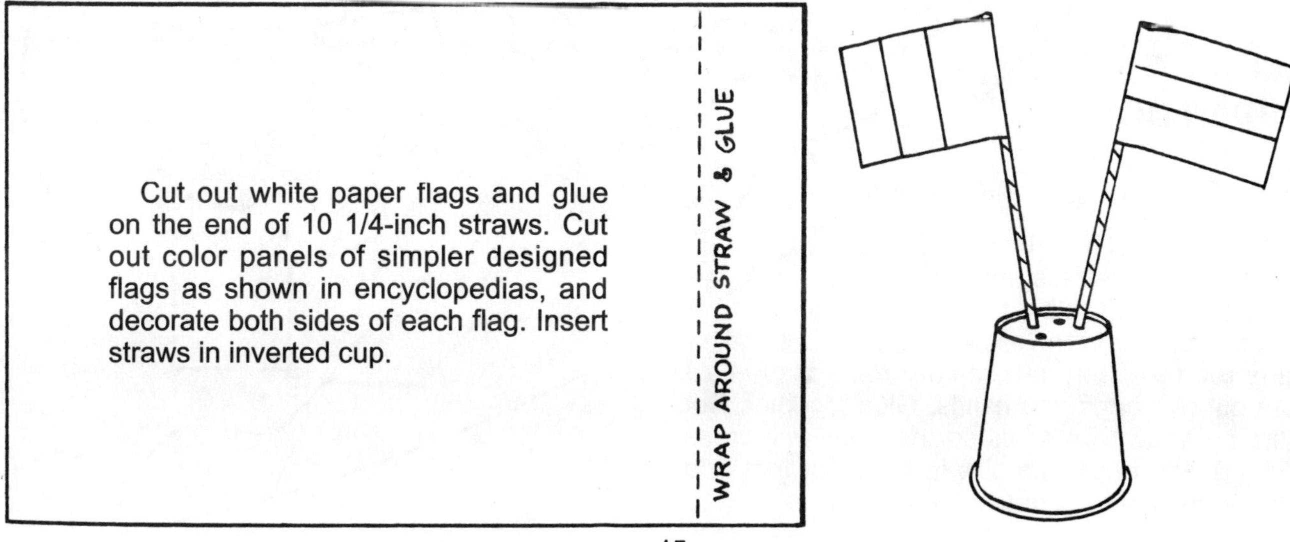

Cut out white paper flags and glue on the end of 10 1/4-inch straws. Cut out color panels of simpler designed flags as shown in encyclopedias, and decorate both sides of each flag. Insert straws in inverted cup.

WRAP AROUND STRAW & GLUE

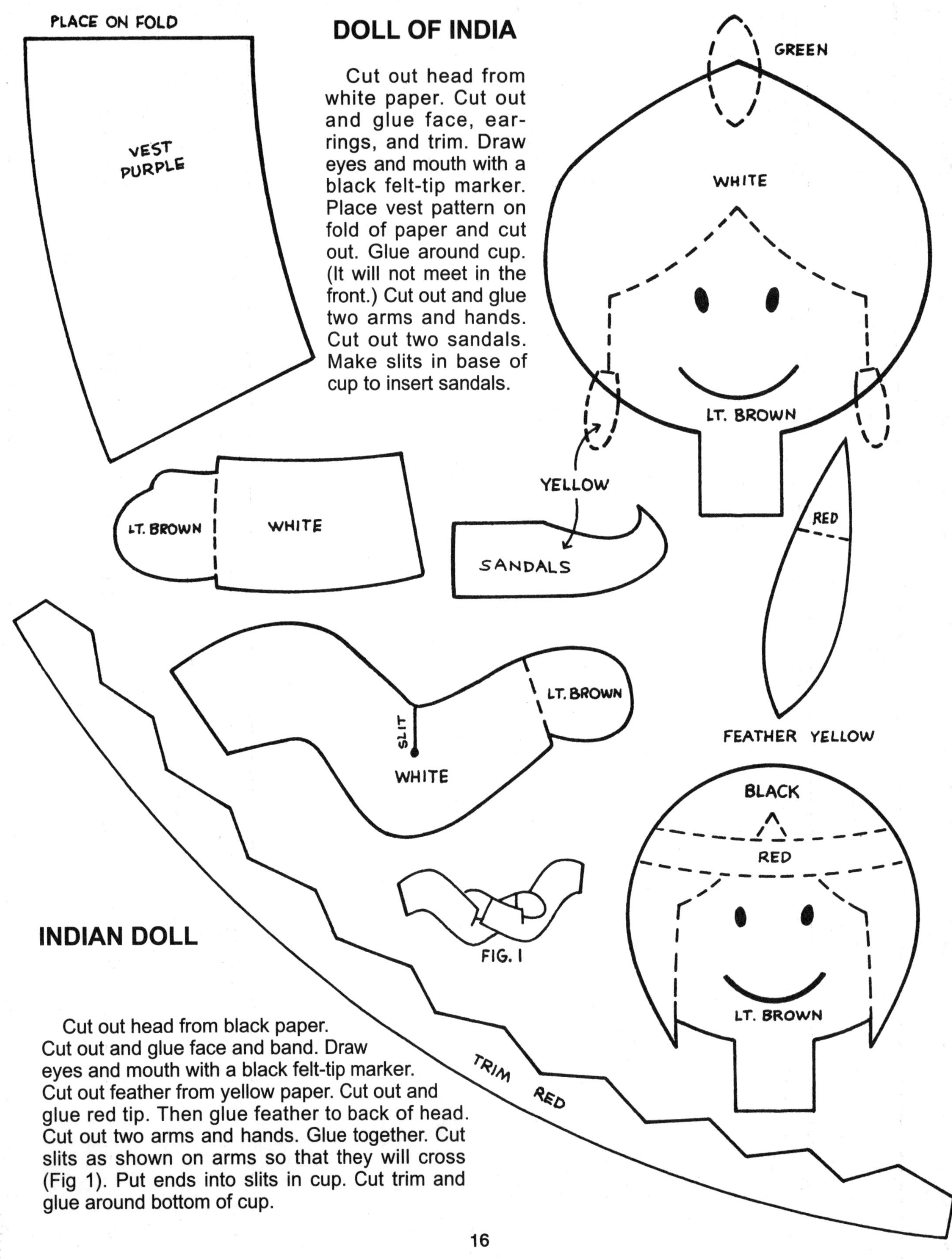

DOLL OF INDIA

Cut out head from white paper. Cut out and glue face, earrings, and trim. Draw eyes and mouth with a black felt-tip marker. Place vest pattern on fold of paper and cut out. Glue around cup. (It will not meet in the front.) Cut out and glue two arms and hands. Cut out two sandals. Make slits in base of cup to insert sandals.

INDIAN DOLL

Cut out head from black paper. Cut out and glue face and band. Draw eyes and mouth with a black felt-tip marker. Cut out feather from yellow paper. Cut out and glue red tip. Then glue feather to back of head. Cut out two arms and hands. Glue together. Cut slits as shown on arms so that they will cross (Fig 1). Put ends into slits in cup. Cut trim and glue around bottom of cup.

HAWAIIAN DOLL

Cut out head from black paper. Cut out and glue face and flower. Draw eyes and mouth with a black felt-tip marker. Cut out leis with pinking shears (if available) and glue on body cup. Cut out two arms and insert in body slits. Cut out skirt of yellow tissue paper. Fringe skirt and glue around cup at the waist only.

AFRICAN DOLL

Cut out head from black paper. Cut out and glue face and earrings. Draw eyes and mouth with a black felt-tip marker. Cut out arms and glue to body cup. Cut out shield and stripes. Glue together, and then glue the shield over the arm.

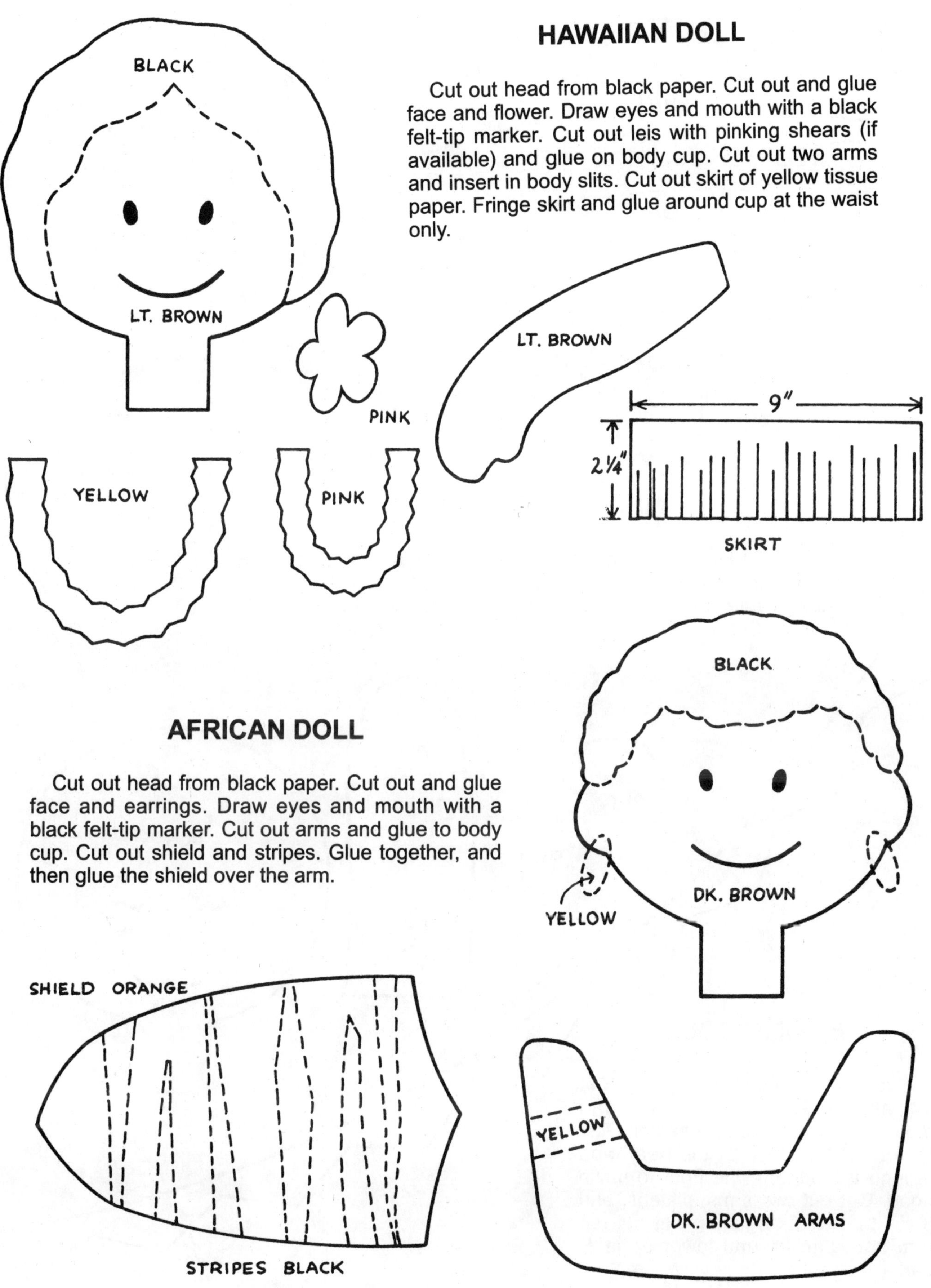

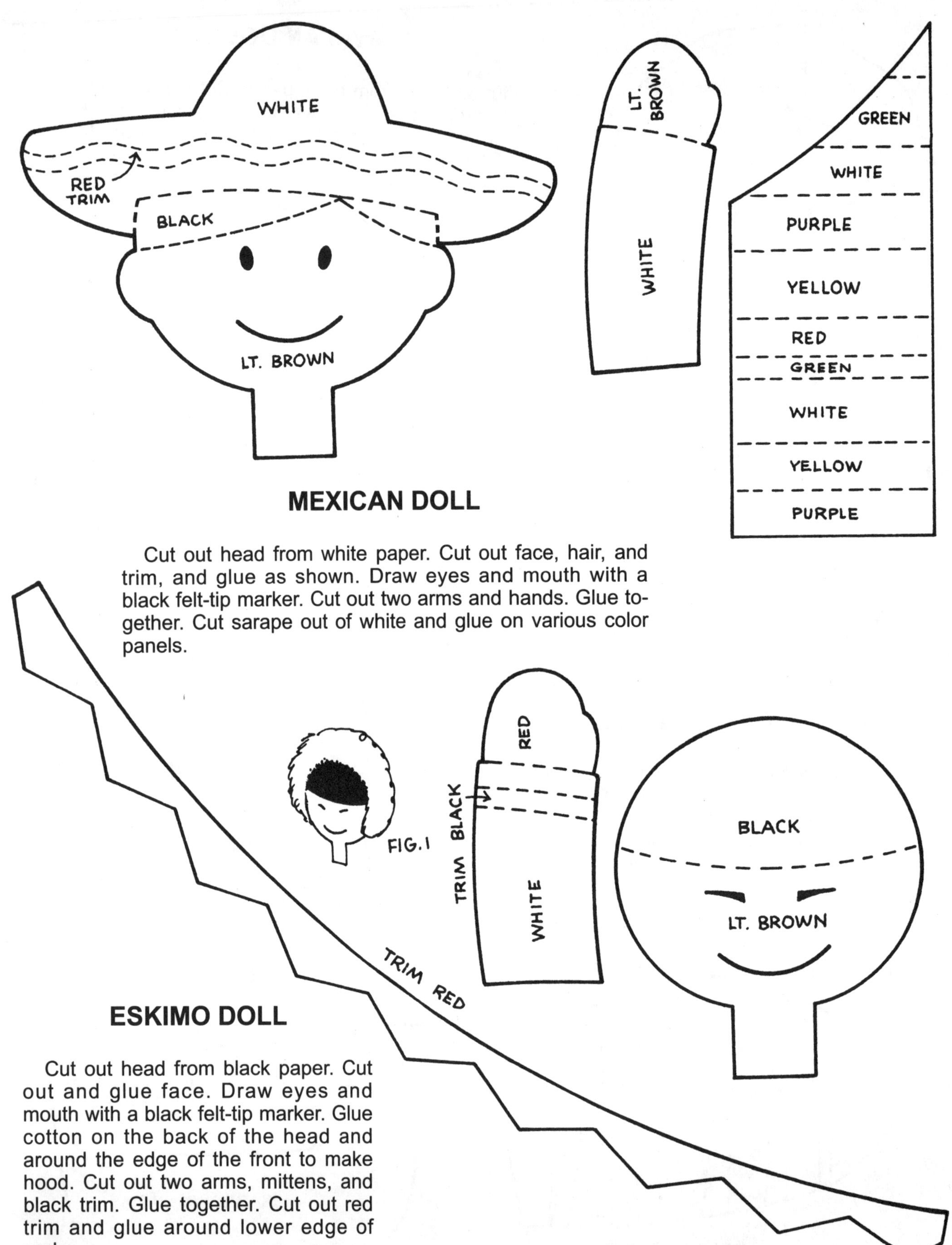

MEXICAN DOLL

Cut out head from white paper. Cut out face, hair, and trim, and glue as shown. Draw eyes and mouth with a black felt-tip marker. Cut out two arms and hands. Glue together. Cut sarape out of white and glue on various color panels.

ESKIMO DOLL

Cut out head from black paper. Cut out and glue face. Draw eyes and mouth with a black felt-tip marker. Glue cotton on the back of the head and around the edge of the front to make hood. Cut out two arms, mittens, and black trim. Glue together. Cut out red trim and glue around lower edge of parka.

RUSSIAN DOLL

Cut out head from tan paper. Place hat pattern on fold and cut out. Glue on hat at an angle with the head between the folded paper. Draw eyes and mouth with a black felt-tip marker. Cut out two arms and hands. Glue together. Cut out legs and boots. Glue together. Cut slits in sides of cup (Fig. 1) for the legs. Point toes forward to make doll stand.

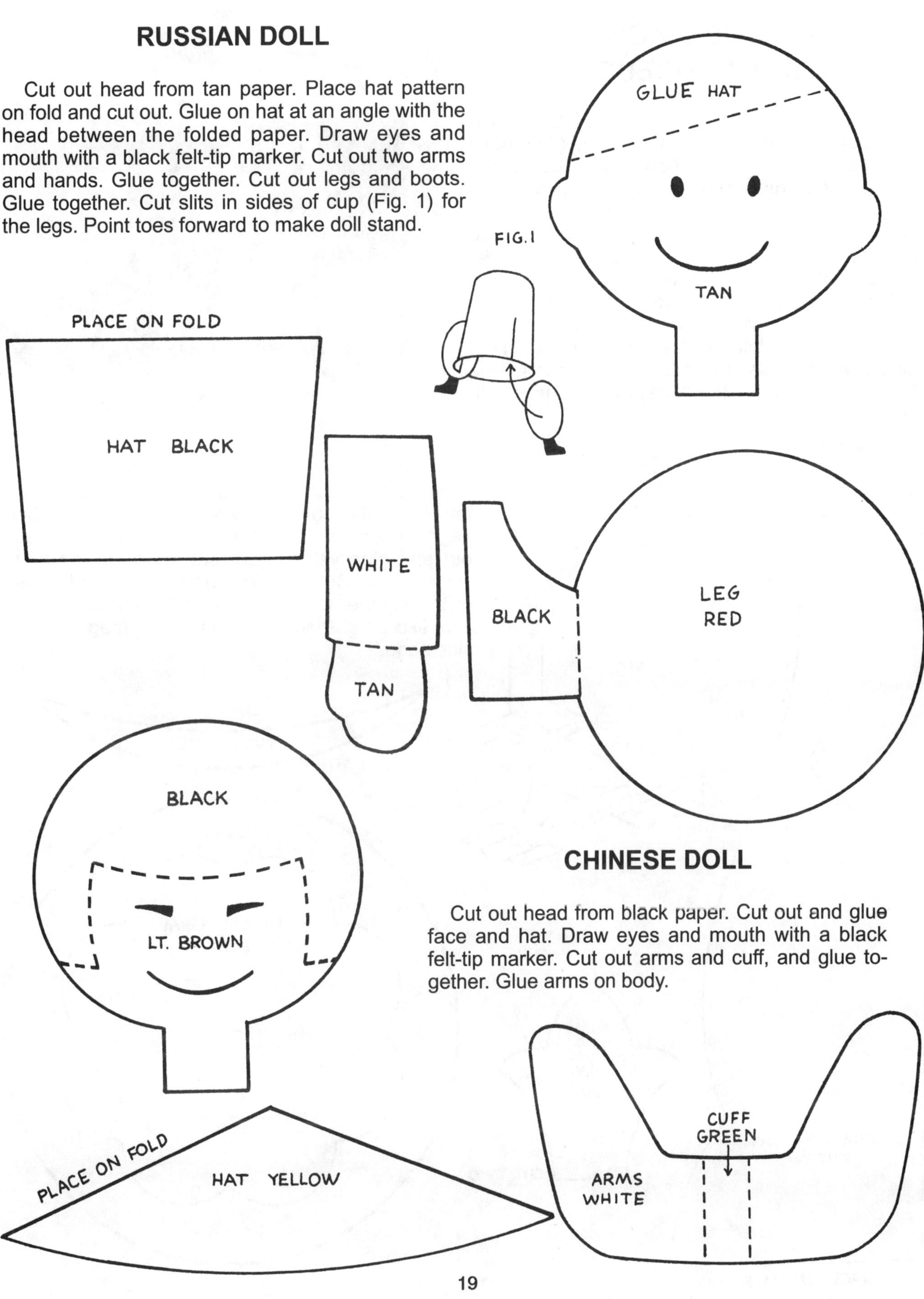

CHINESE DOLL

Cut out head from black paper. Cut out and glue face and hat. Draw eyes and mouth with a black felt-tip marker. Cut out arms and cuff, and glue together. Glue arms on body.

CIRCUS WAGON CENTERPIECE

Material needed: cardboard shoe box, 2 large plastic straws, 4 cardboard ribbon spools (they need not be empty), construction paper, lace paper doily, 4 small rubber bands, scissors, glue

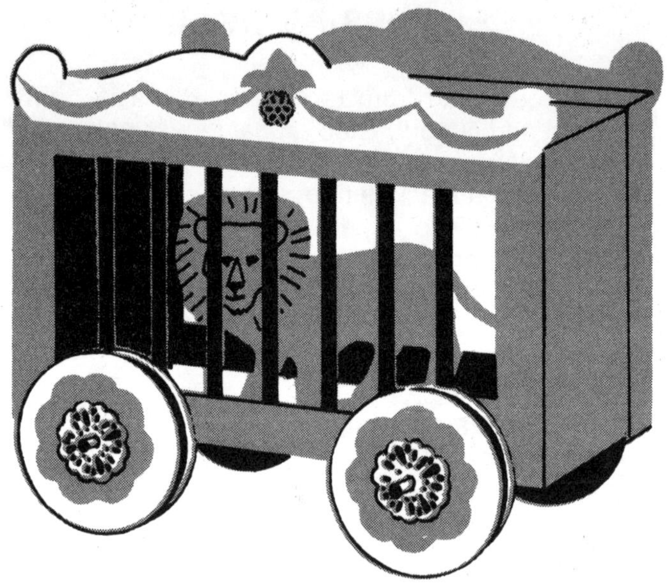

Cover shoe box with blue paper, covering lid separately, so box can be opened to put lion inside. Cut out bottom and top of box, leaving at least a 3/4-inch margin all around (Fig. 1). Glue two 2-inch squares of paper on side of box that will form bottom of wagon (folding first as shown in Fig. 1) to hold straws. Wheels are made by covering one side of ribbon spools (Fig. 2) with yellow circle, then with blue trim.

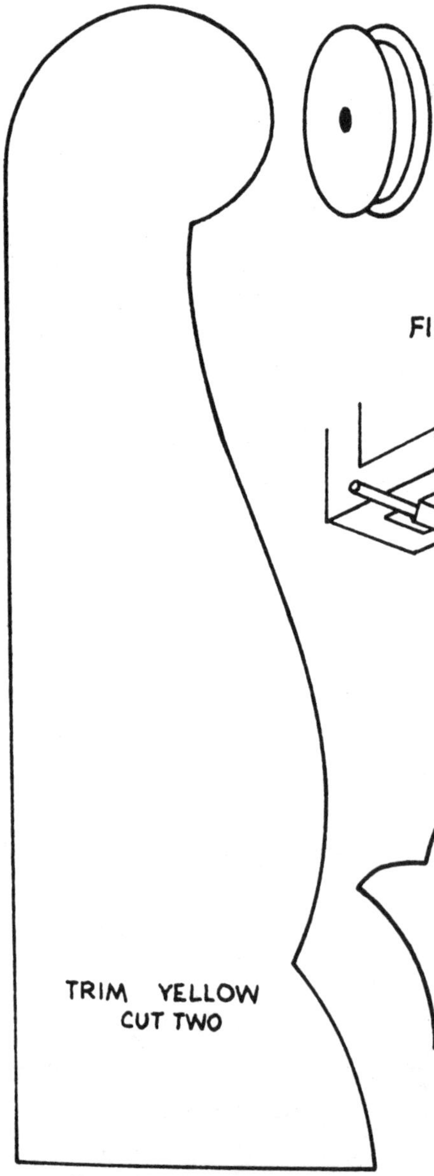

PLACE ON FOLD

FIG. 2

FIG. 1

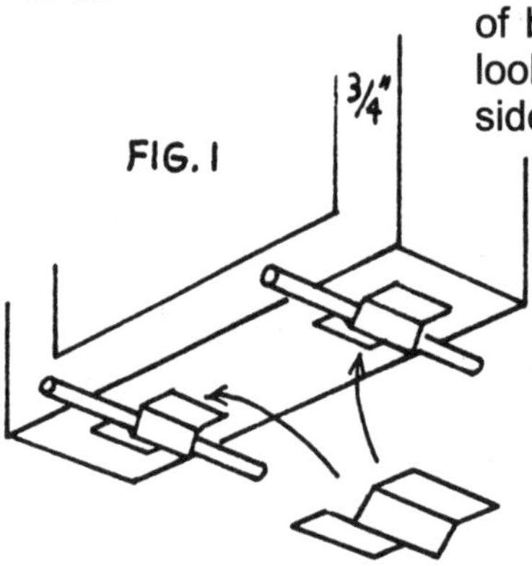

Cut out circular design from doily and glue in center of wheels. Insert ends of straw through center of wheels. Cut off excess length. Wrap rubber bands around ends of straw to hold wheels on. Cut out and glue yellow, red, and blue trim on both sides of box. Cut 14 strips (1/4 inch x 4 3/4 inches) of black paper to glue on inside of box opening to look like bars. Place a lion stand-up (page 21) inside cage.

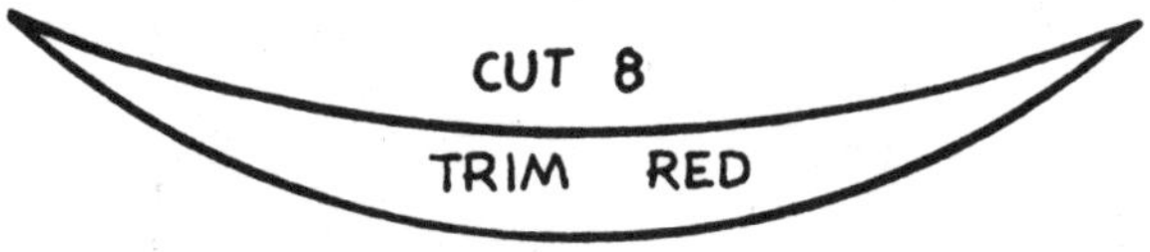

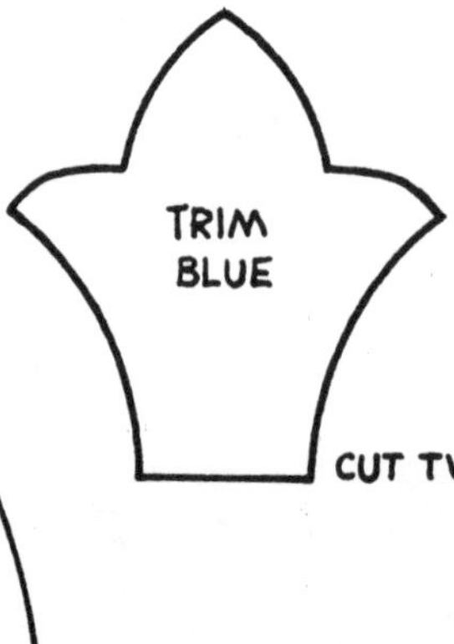

CUT TWO

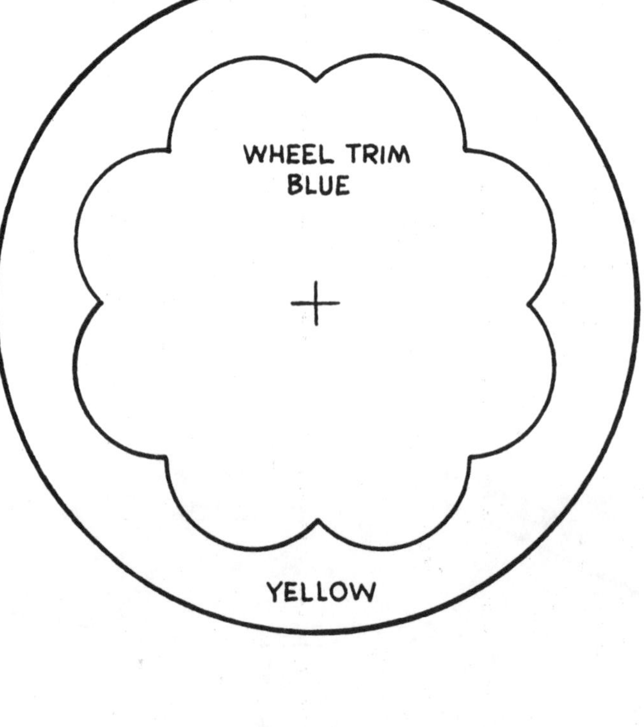

LION STAND-UP

Material needed: construction paper, chenille wire, tan crepe paper, scissors, glue

Place pattern of lion body on fold of paper and cut out. Cut out head. Cut out and glue on nose and ears. Draw eyes, nose, and mouth with a black felt-tip marker. Cut out mane by placing pattern on fold of crepe paper. Cut slits around the edge. Glue face on, then glue 2-inch length of chenille wire in between mane. Glue end of chenille wire in hole in body (Fig. 1). Glue 4-inch length of chenille wire in body for tail.

This lion may be used with the circus wagon centerpiece on page 20.

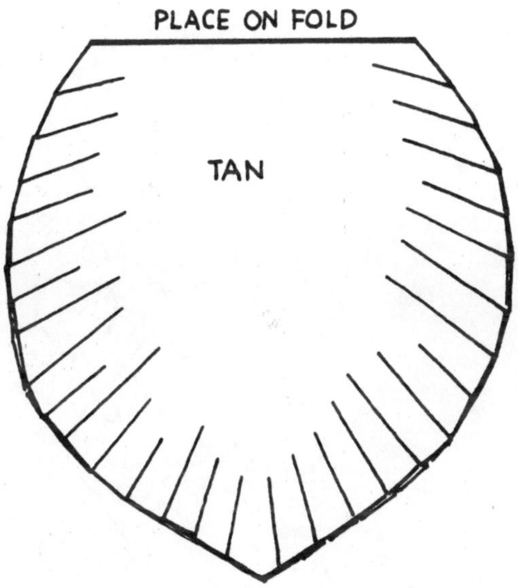

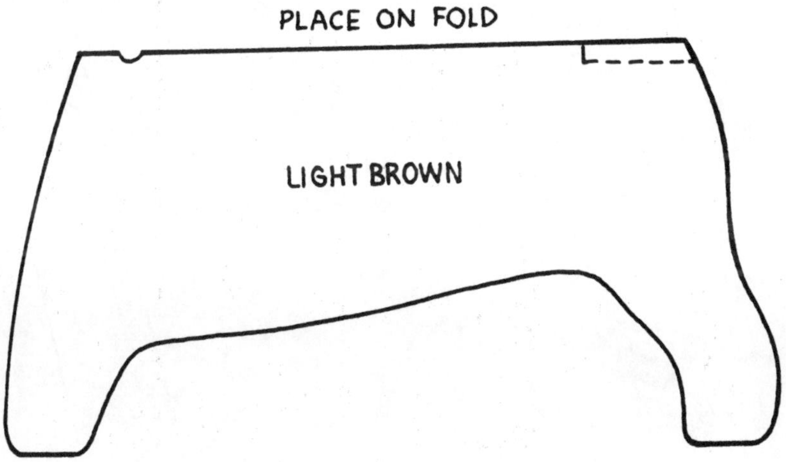

GINGERBREAD HOUSE CENTERPIECE

Material needed: construction paper, paper straw, white lace paper doily, glue, marshmallows (large and small), toothpicks, scissors

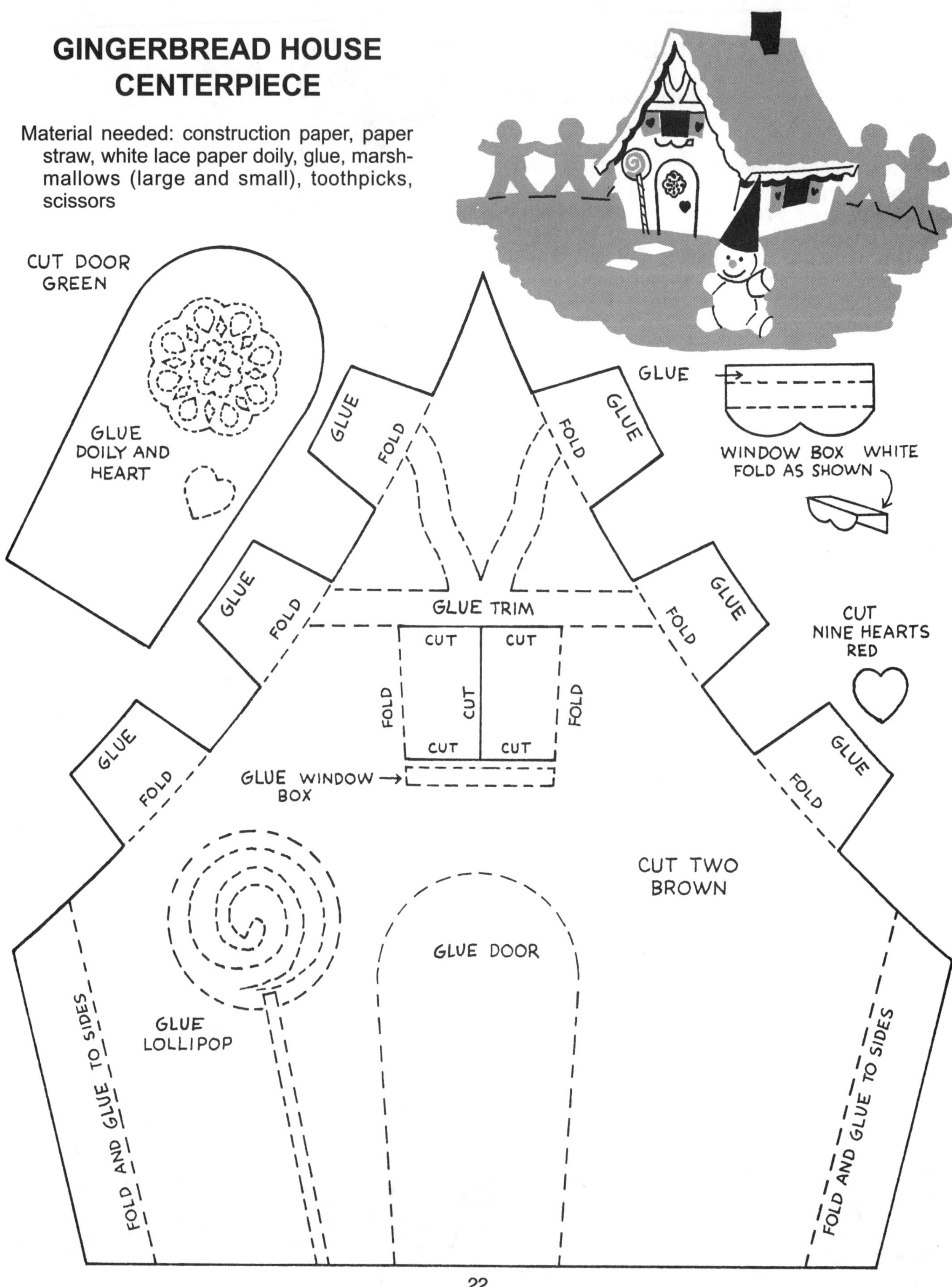

Cut out front and back of house. Cut window slits and fold shutters out. Cut out door, window box, hearts, shutters, pink trim, white lollipop, and red swirl. Glue swirl to lollipop. Attach 2-inch pink straw (Fig. 1). Glue door, shutters, window box, trim, lollipop, and hearts to front. On back of house, glue shutters and hearts. Cut circle from doily and glue to door. Cut out two sides of house. Cut slits for windows, and fold out. Glue on shutters and hearts. Glue sides to front and back (Fig. 2). Fold 9-inch by 12-inch green paper in half and glue on for roof (Fig. 2). Cut out chimney, fold (Fig. 3), and glue on roof. Cut out two 9-inch and four 6-inch pieces of white trim and glue around edge of roof (Fig. 2). Make marshmallow man and cut out paper dolls to add to centerpiece, if desired.

WHITE TRIM

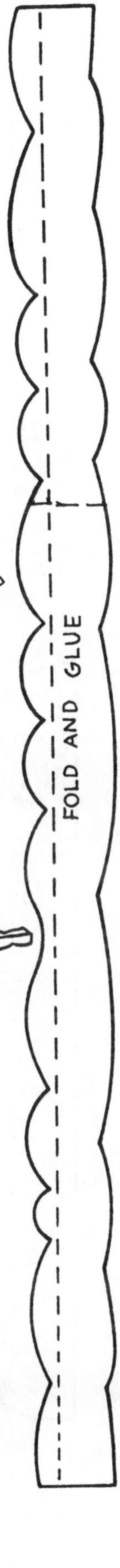

CUT
EIGHT SHUTTERS
GREEN

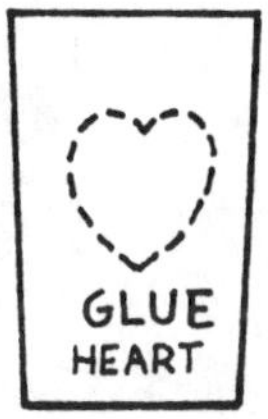

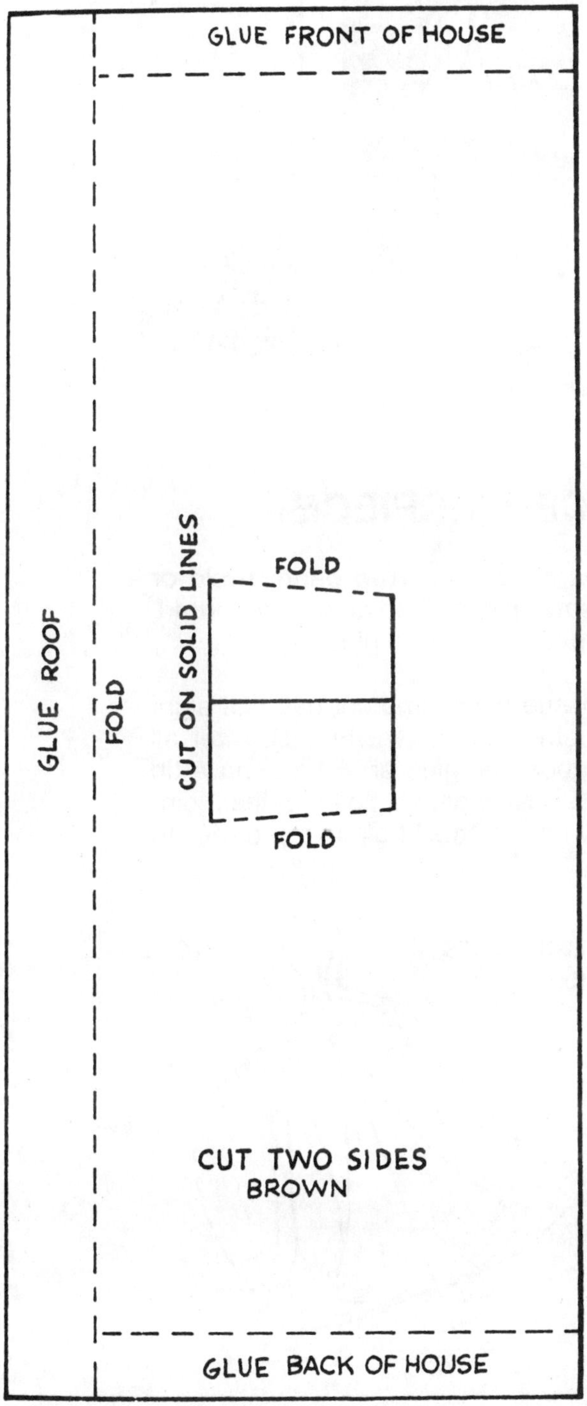

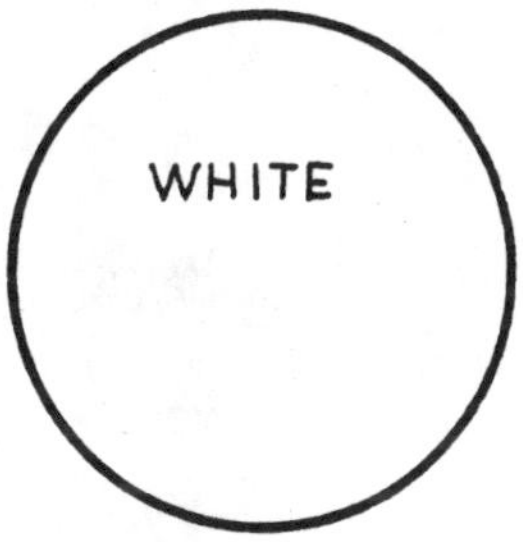

SLIT

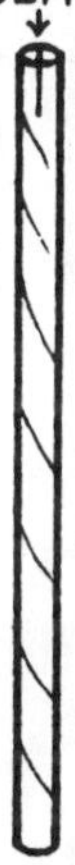

PINK STRAW

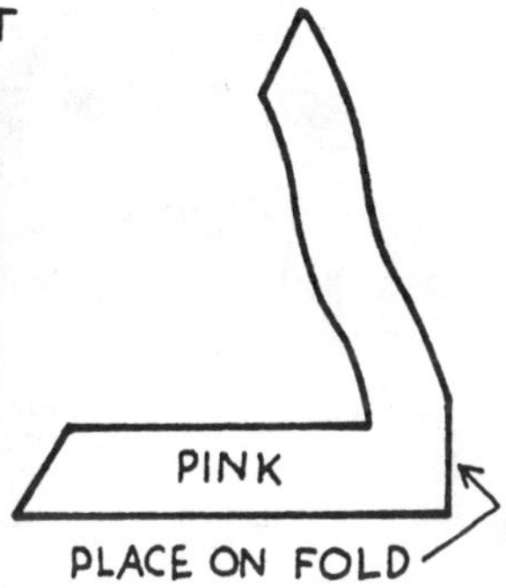

RED

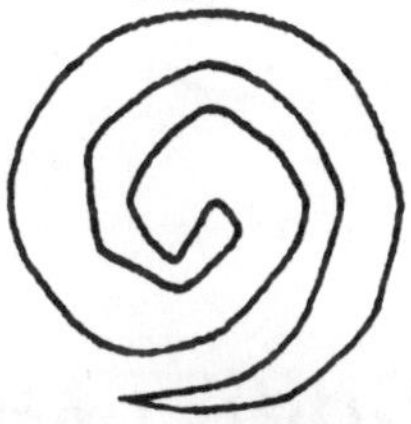

FIG. 1

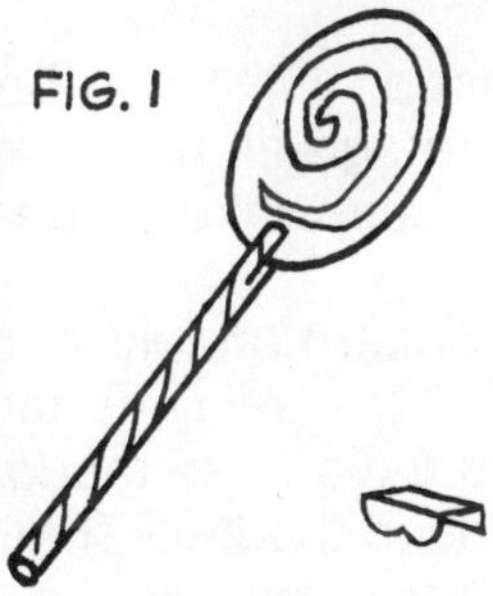

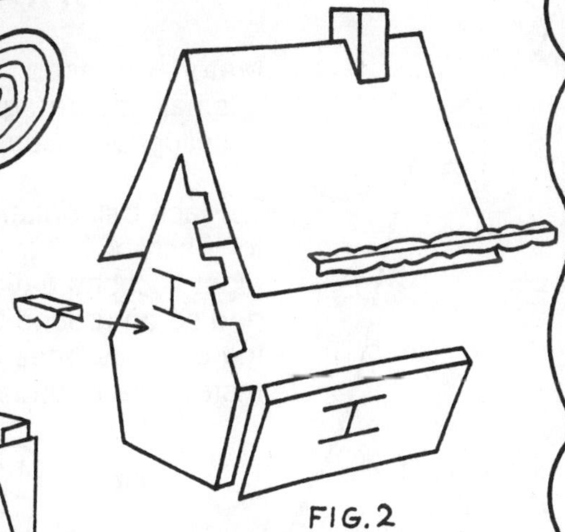

FIG. 2

FIG. 3

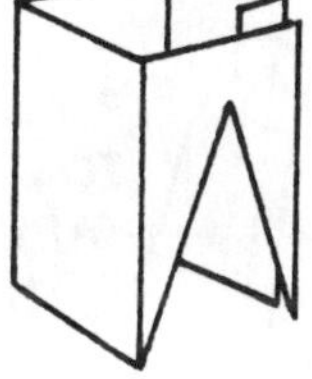

CHIMNEY
FOLD ON DOTTED LINES

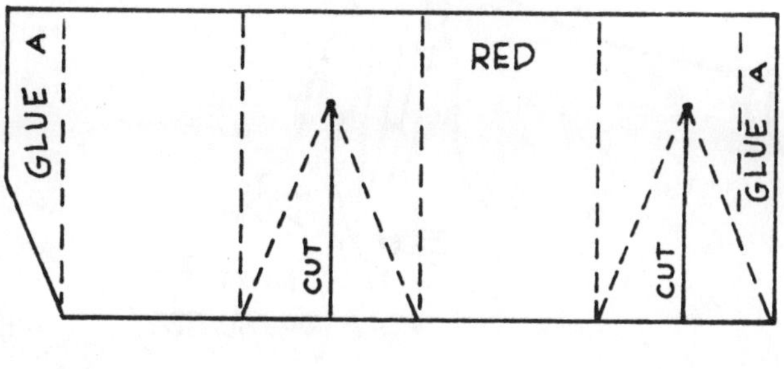

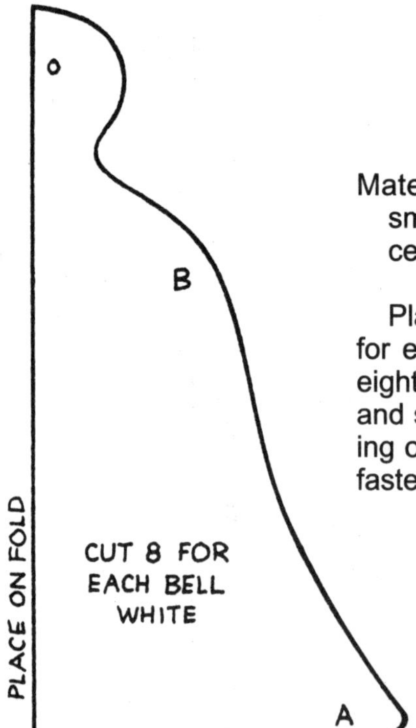

CHRISTMAS CENTERPIECE

Material needed: white cardboard, foil gift wrap paper (gold or small pattern), green ribbon, small piece of florist wire or thread, cellophane tape, white tissue paper, scissors, glue

Place bell pattern on fold of tissue paper and cut out. Cut eight for each bell. Tape sections together as shown (Fig. 1). After all eight sections have been taped together, glue an A tip to an A tip and so on around the bells (Fig. 2). Now glue B tips together, joining opposite ones from the A's. Make a small hole in top of bell to fasten wire or thread.

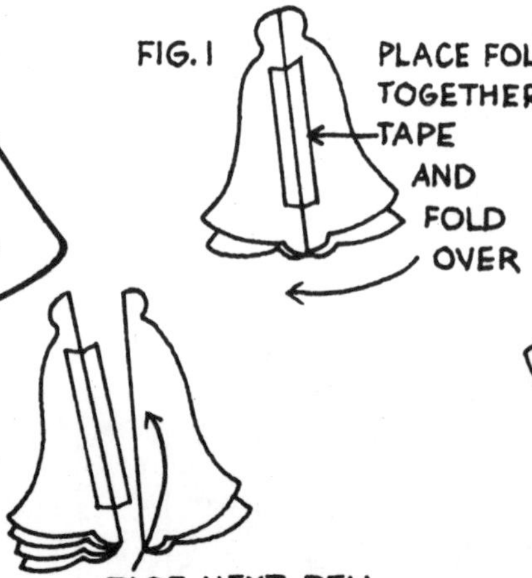

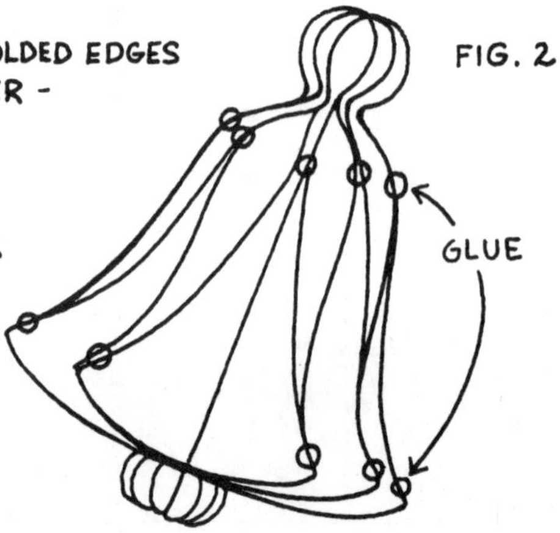

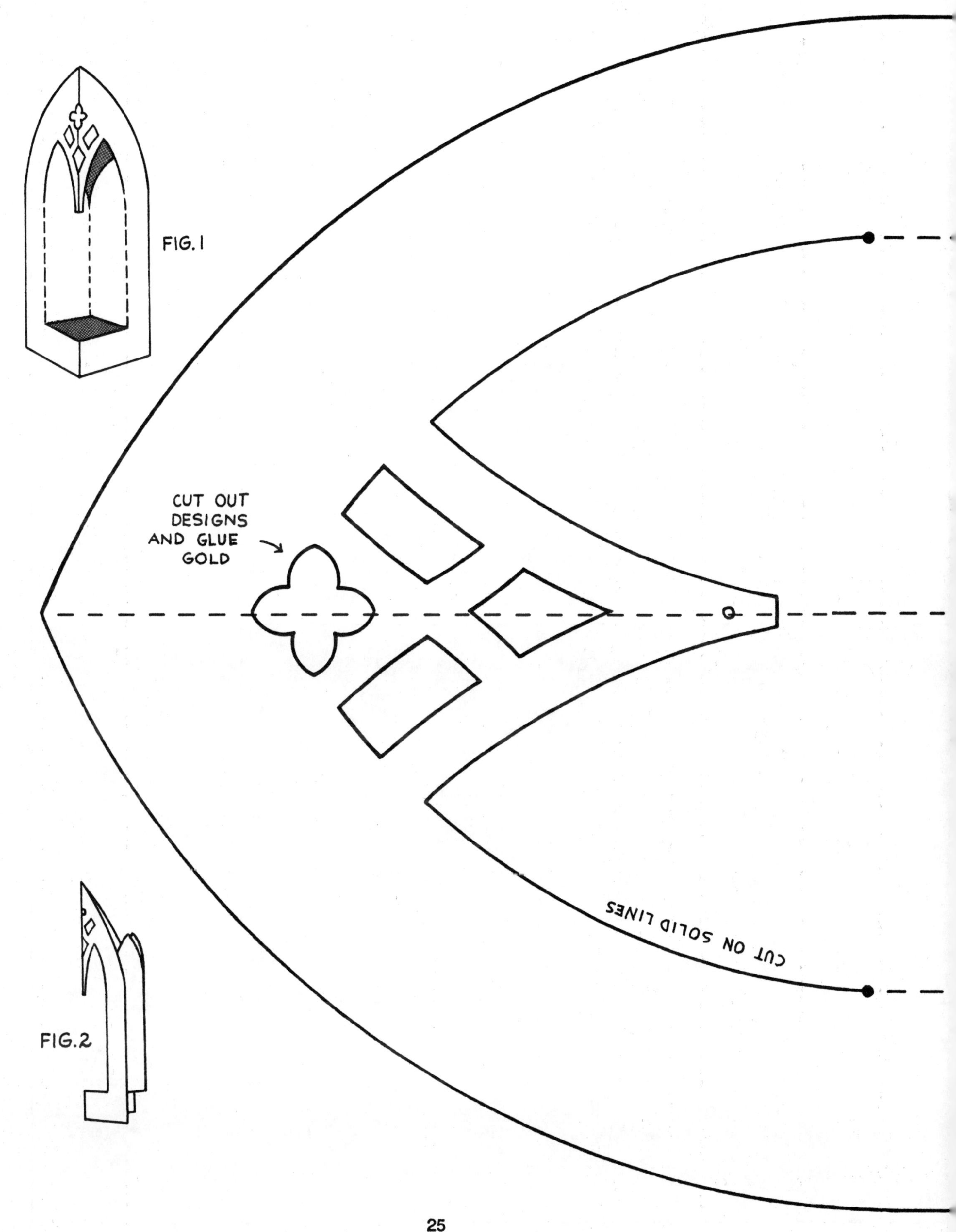

FIG. 1
FIG. 2
CUT OUT DESIGNS AND GLUE GOLD
CUT ON SOLID LINES

A

Cut out window design pattern from white cardboard (not too heavy, but firm enough to stand). Fold and stand as shown (Figs. 1 and 2). Put glue on the inverted middle section from A to C and glue foil paper. Cut out gold designs and glue on. Make three windows for triptych shown on page 24. Hang bells with wire and tie green bows to cover the wire. The addition of pine cones and evergreen boughs would add to the triptych. Or place window sections back to back to form a circle and make a wreath of evergreens in front of them, with small green votive candles for sparkle.

B

CUT ON SOLID LINES

C

FOLD ON DOTTED LINES A B C

MANGER SCENE

Material needed: construction paper, scissors, glue

Cut out two figures of Joseph, and glue together from the waist up. Leave the lower half free to be spread open, allowing the figure to stand. Cut out head, hair, hands, gown, and staff, and glue in place.

Cut out two figures of Mary, and glue top half together. Cut out veil, and glue on. Cut out hands and face, and glue to figure.

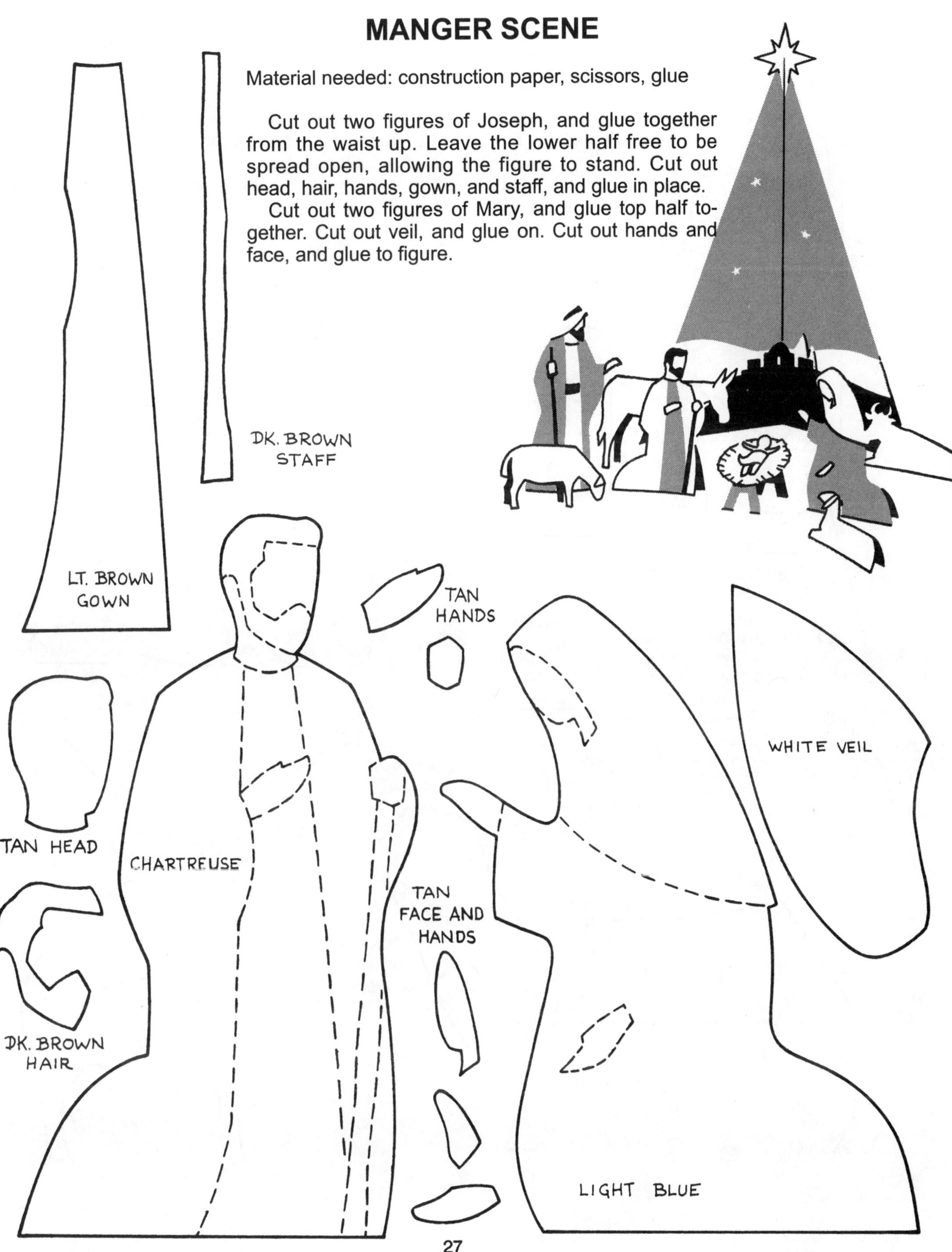

27

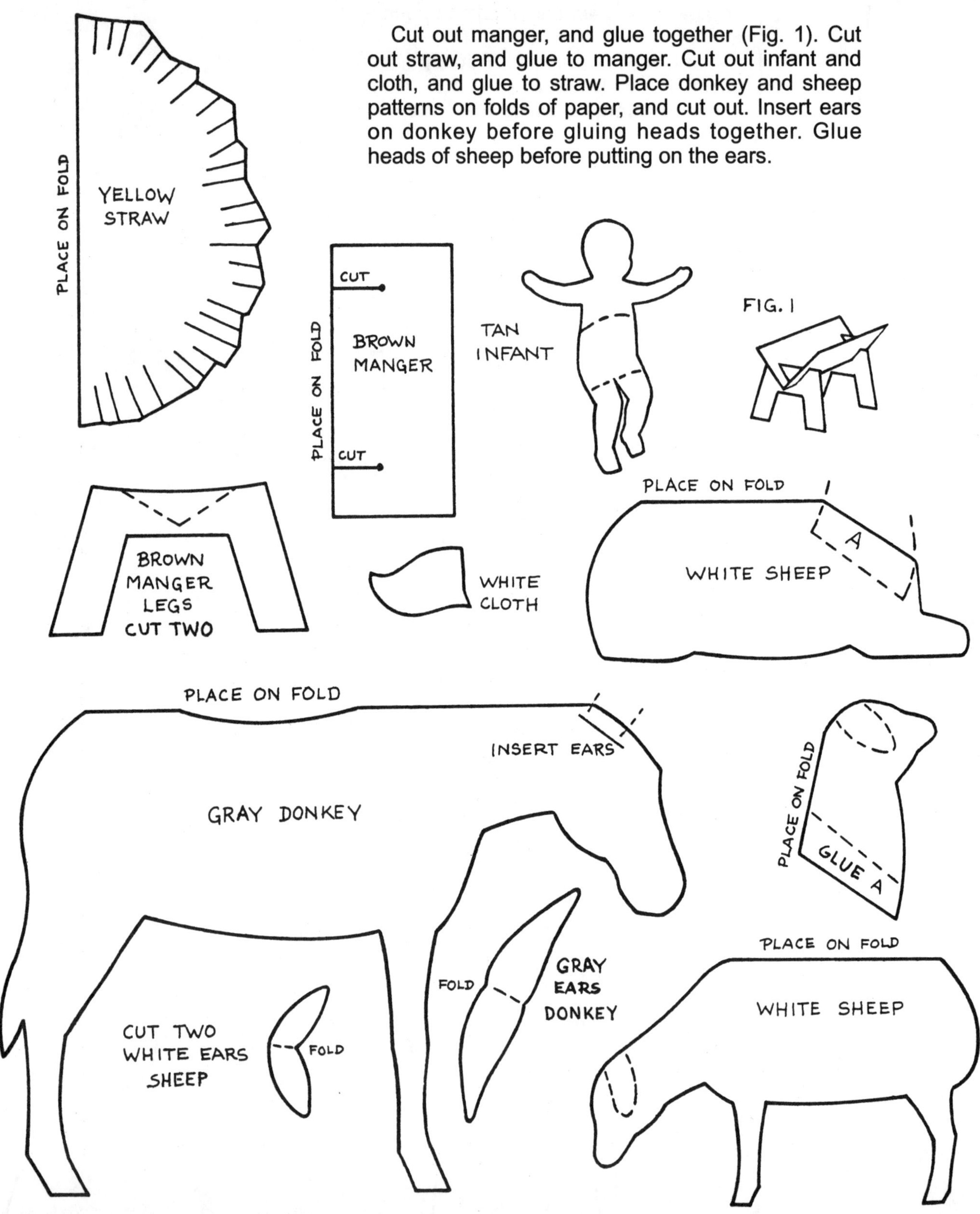

Cut out manger, and glue together (Fig. 1). Cut out straw, and glue to manger. Cut out infant and cloth, and glue to straw. Place donkey and sheep patterns on folds of paper, and cut out. Insert ears on donkey before gluing heads together. Glue heads of sheep before putting on the ears.

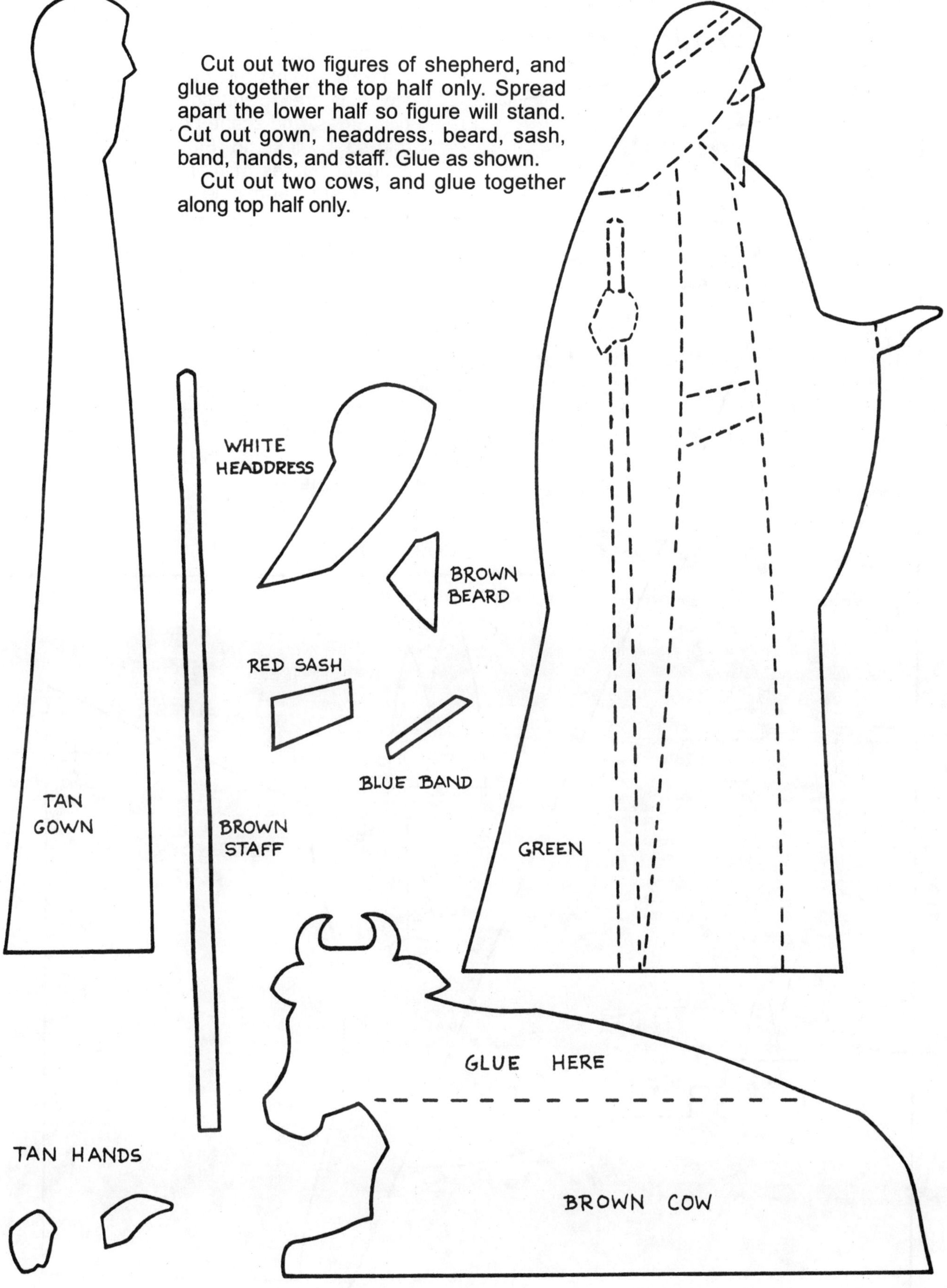

Cut out two figures of shepherd, and glue together the top half only. Spread apart the lower half so figure will stand. Cut out gown, headdress, beard, sash, band, hands, and staff. Glue as shown.
Cut out two cows, and glue together along top half only.
WHITE HEADDRESS
BROWN BEARD
RED SASH
BLUE BAND
TAN GOWN
BROWN STAFF
GREEN
TAN HANDS
GLUE HERE
BROWN COW

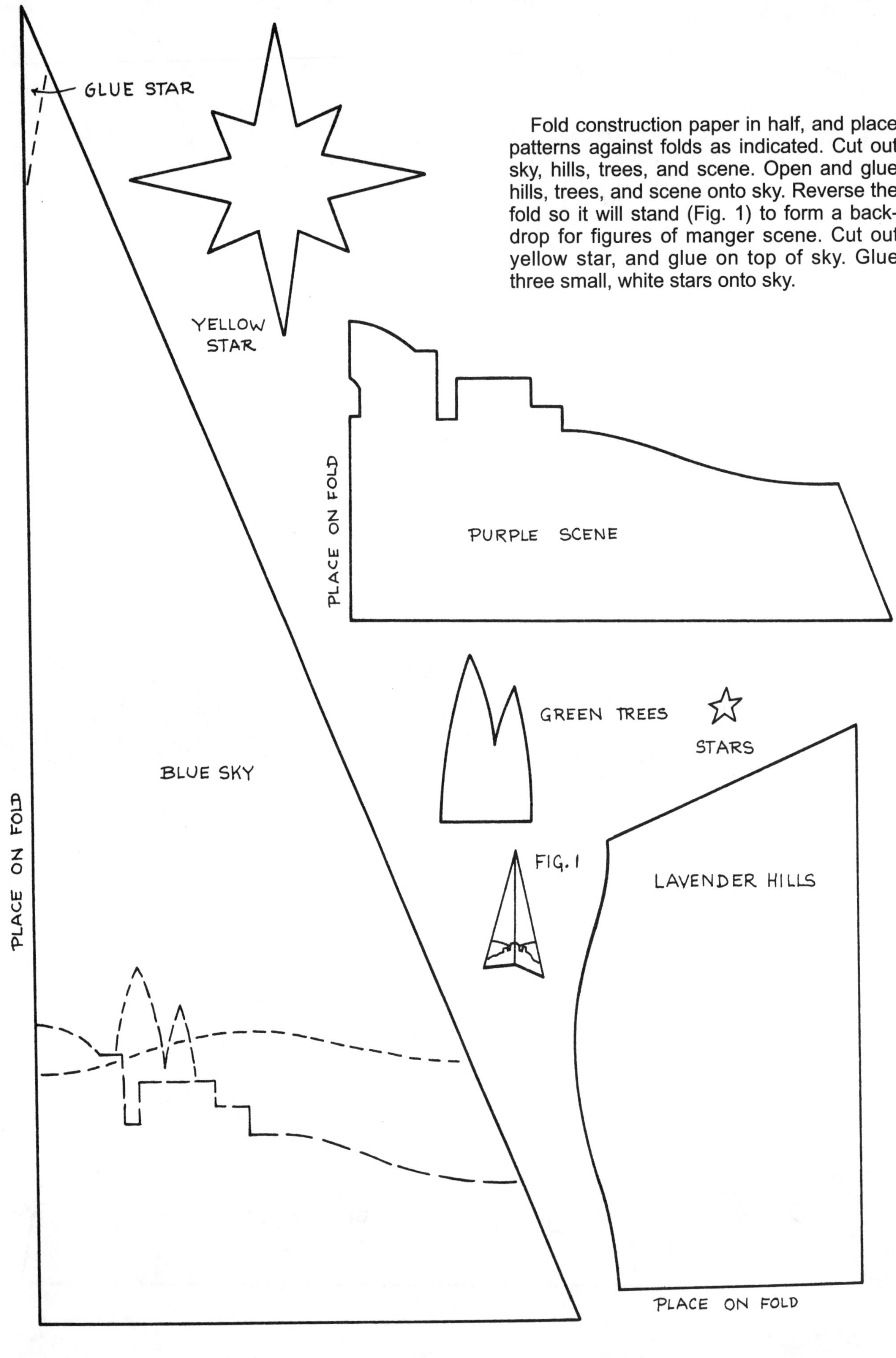

Fold construction paper in half, and place patterns against folds as indicated. Cut out sky, hills, trees, and scene. Open and glue hills, trees, and scene onto sky. Reverse the fold so it will stand (Fig. 1) to form a backdrop for figures of manger scene. Cut out yellow star, and glue on top of sky. Glue three small, white stars onto sky.

WISE-MEN FOLLOWING THE STAR

Material needed: construction paper, scissors, glue

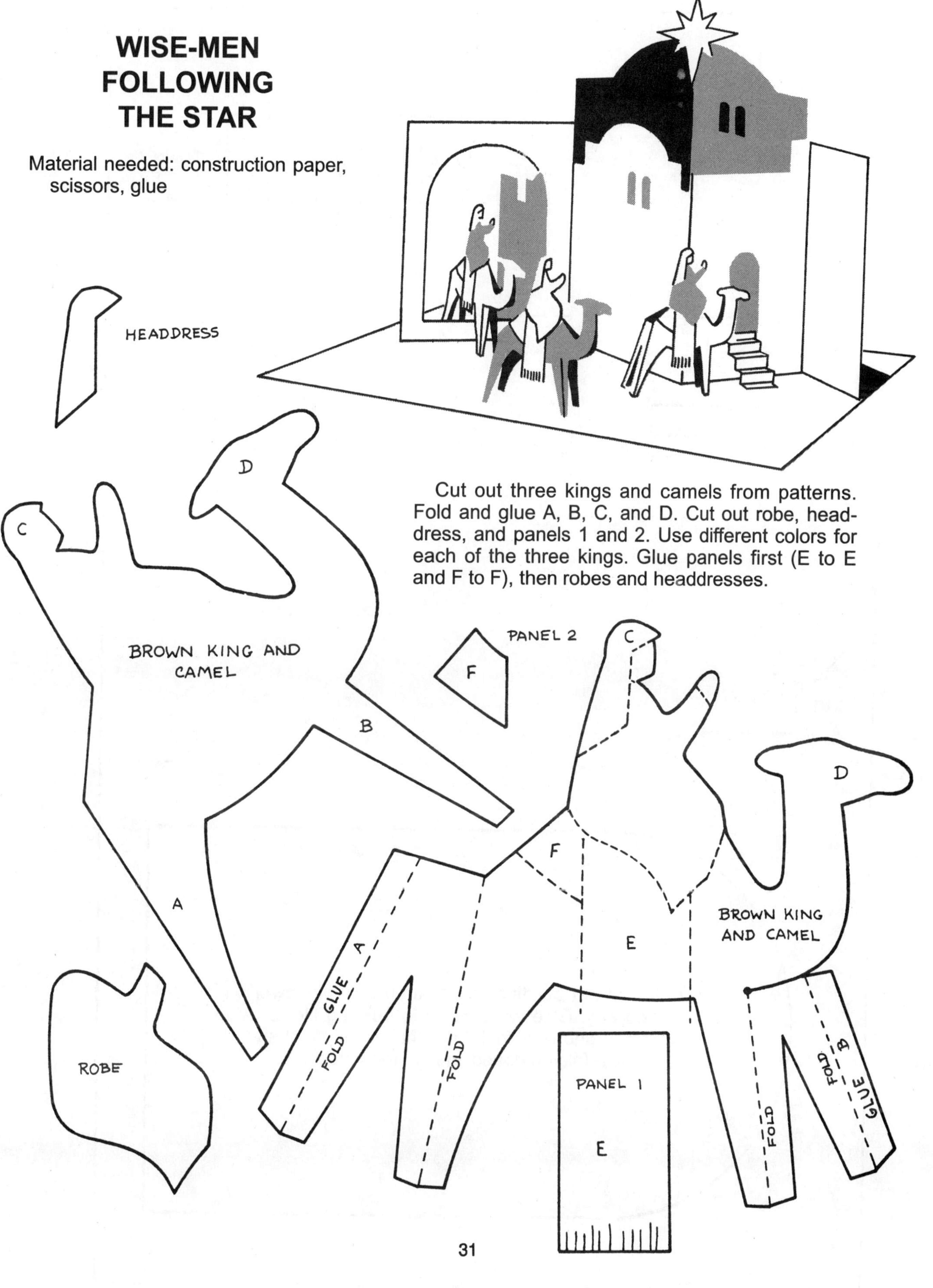

Cut out three kings and camels from patterns. Fold and glue A, B, C, and D. Cut out robe, head-dress, and panels 1 and 2. Use different colors for each of the three kings. Glue panels first (E to E and F to F), then robes and headdresses.

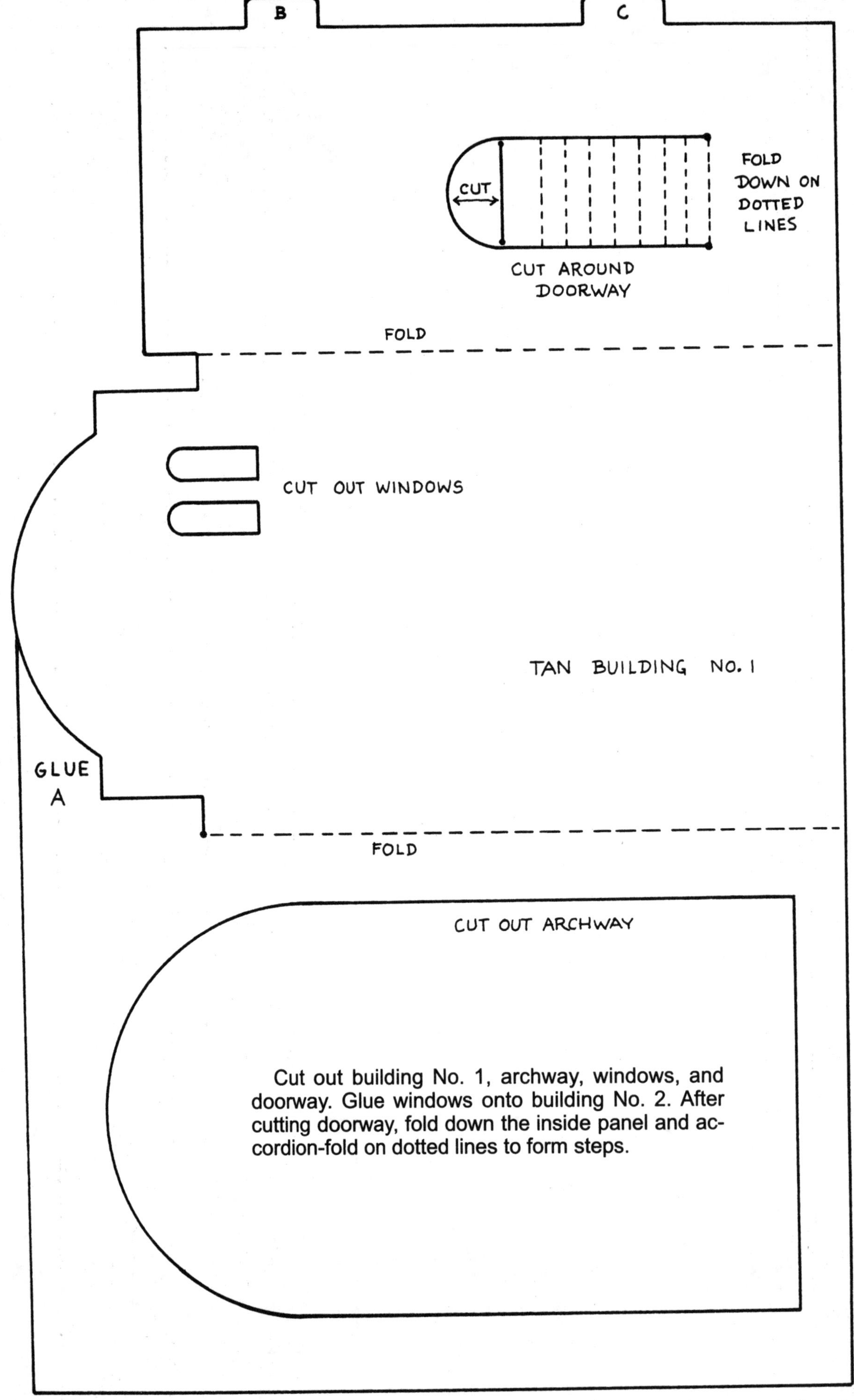

Cut out building No. 1, archway, windows, and doorway. Glue windows onto building No. 2. After cutting doorway, fold down the inside panel and accordion-fold on dotted lines to form steps.

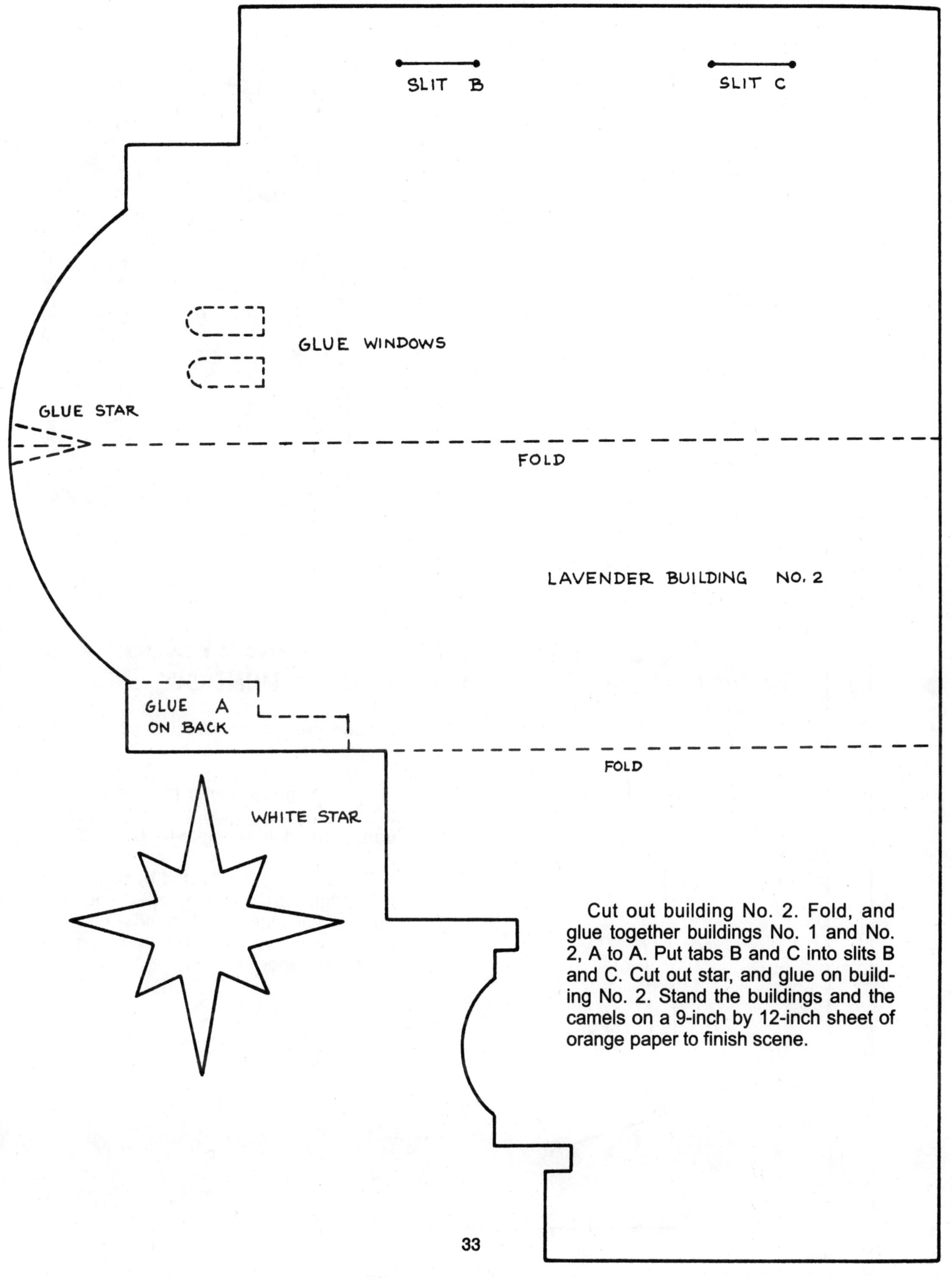

Cut out building No. 2. Fold, and glue together buildings No. 1 and No. 2, A to A. Put tabs B and C into slits B and C. Cut out star, and glue on building No. 2. Stand the buildings and the camels on a 9-inch by 12-inch sheet of orange paper to finish scene.

33

NO. 1

YELLOW CROWN

TAN FACE

YELLOW
CHALICE

TAN HANDS

YELLOW
CHALICE

PURPLE
FIGURE

LAVENDER
PANEL

FOLD

PLACE ON FOLD

THREE KINGS WINDOW

Material needed: construction paper, scissors, glue

Place window frame pattern against the fold of black paper, and cut out. Glue frame to dark-blue paper (9 inches by 11 inches).

To make king No. 1, start by cutting out entire figure from purple paper. Then cut out and glue on panel, hands, chalice, face, and crown. Glue in position on the dark-blue paper.

For king No. 2, start by cutting out white head-dress and robe. Cut out face, hands, ornament, box, and red panel. Glue these in position on dark-blue background. Background will form part of king's robe.

For king No. 3, start by cutting out green robe. Cut out sleeves, hands, vase, and dark-green panel, and glue in position. Next, cut out face, beard, and crown, and glue on king. Position king on the background as shown. Add white stars.

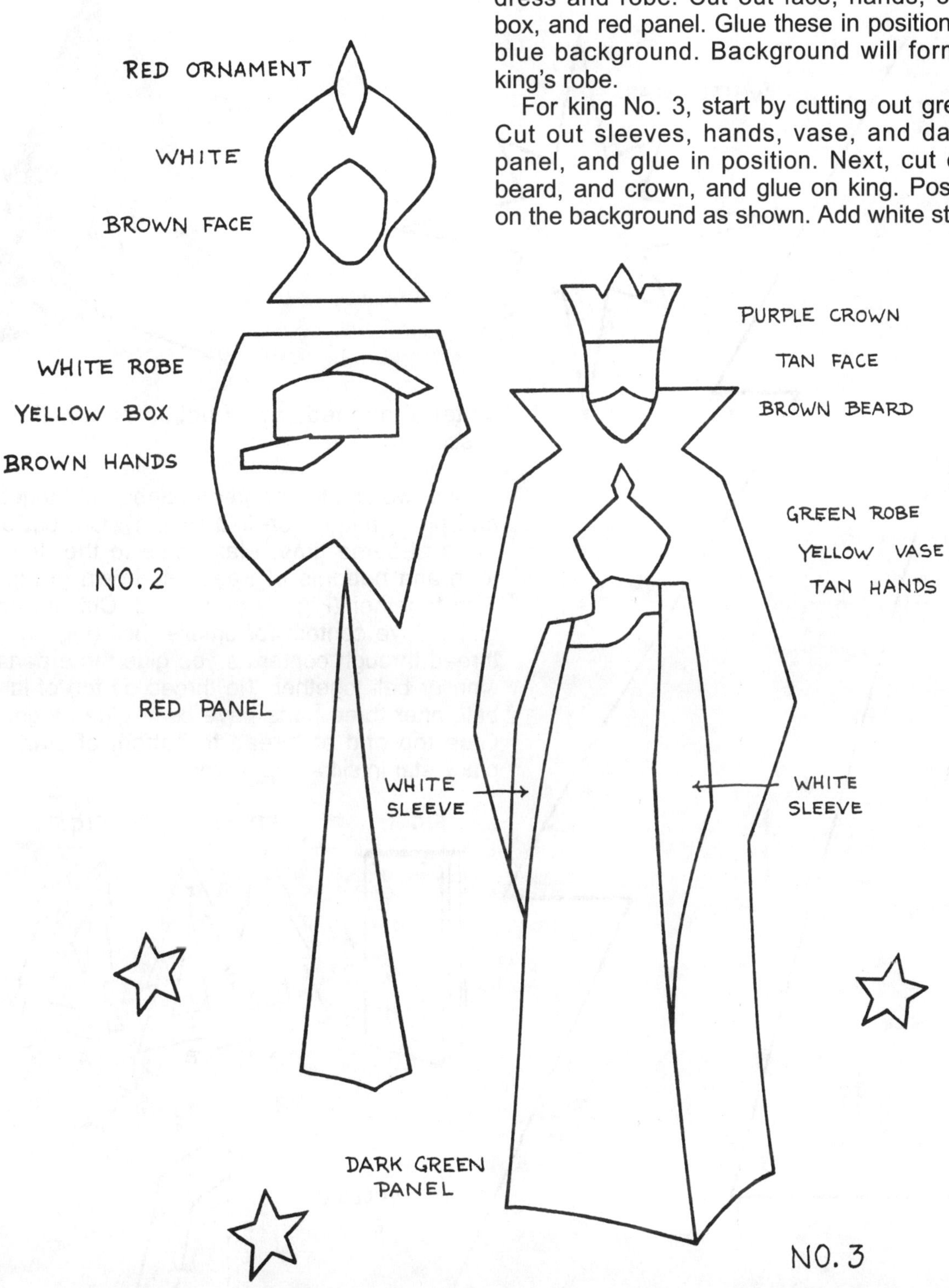

CHRISTMAS TREE WITH BELLS

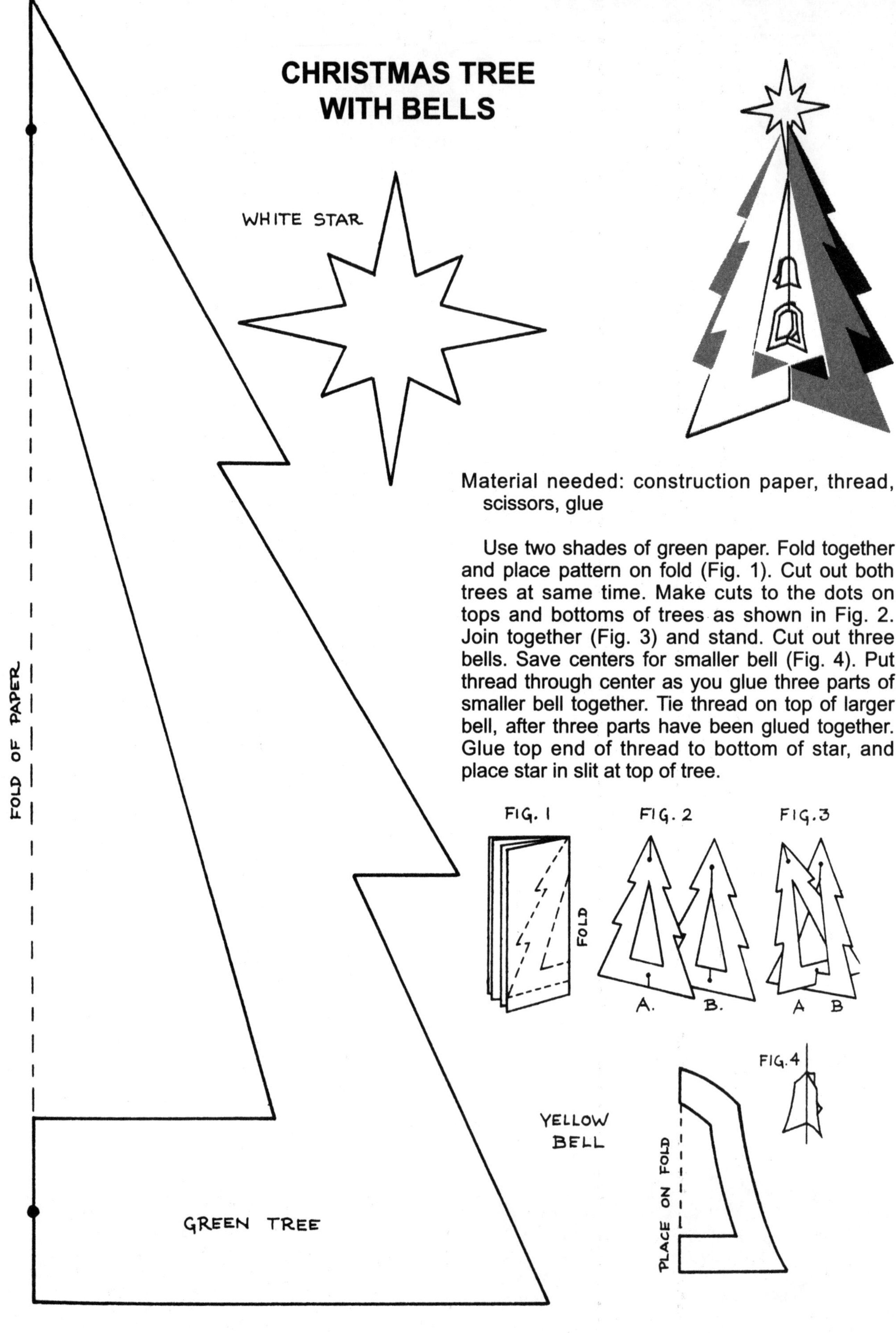

Material needed: construction paper, thread, scissors, glue

Use two shades of green paper. Fold together and place pattern on fold (Fig. 1). Cut out both trees at same time. Make cuts to the dots on tops and bottoms of trees as shown in Fig. 2. Join together (Fig. 3) and stand. Cut out three bells. Save centers for smaller bell (Fig. 4). Put thread through center as you glue three parts of smaller bell together. Tie thread on top of larger bell, after three parts have been glued together. Glue top end of thread to bottom of star, and place star in slit at top of tree.

STAR
OF
BETHLEHEM

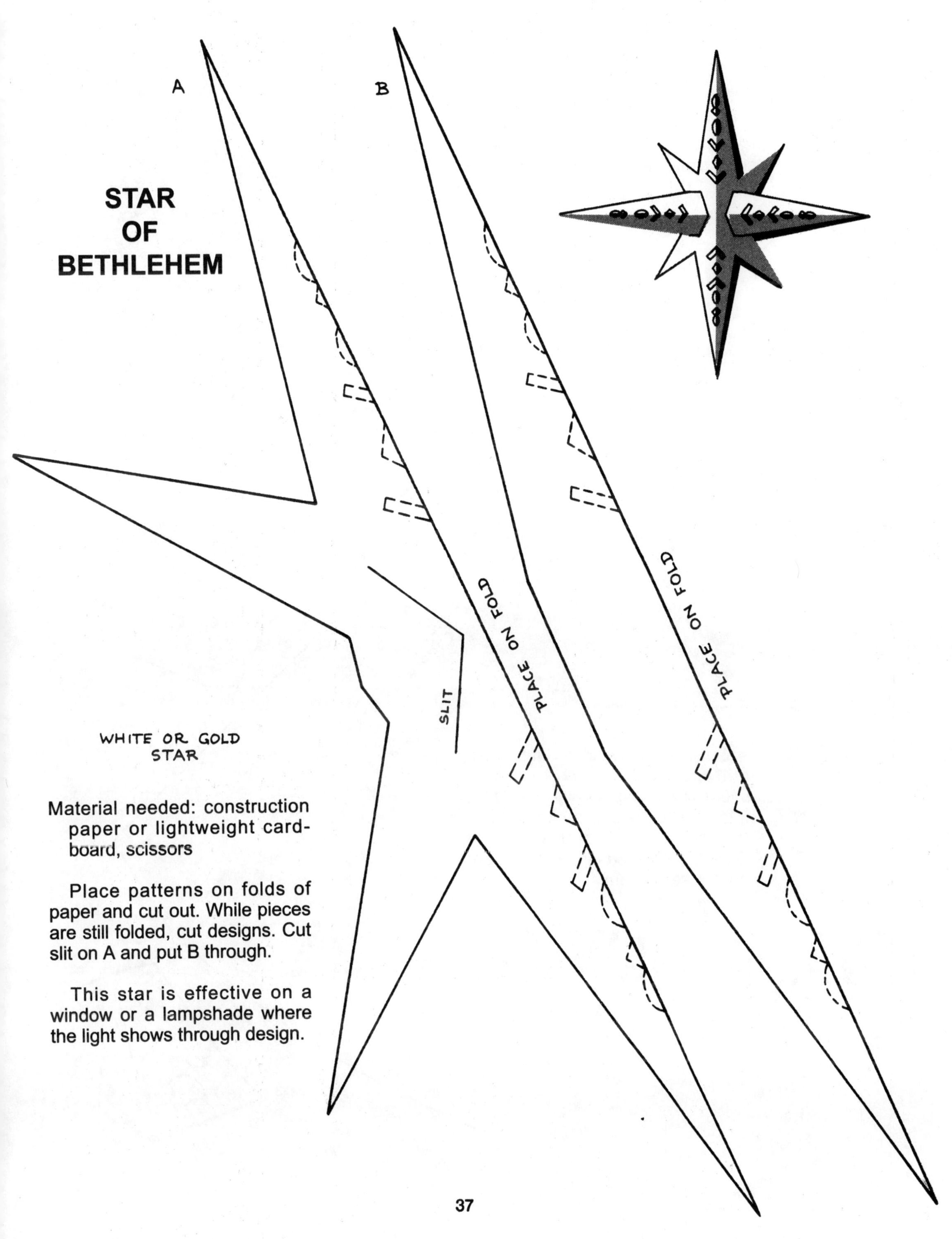

WHITE OR GOLD
STAR

Material needed: construction
paper or lightweight cardboard, scissors

Place patterns on folds of
paper and cut out. While pieces
are still folded, cut designs. Cut
slit on A and put B through.

This star is effective on a
window or a lampshade where
the light shows through design.

POPCORN
CHRISTMAS TREE

Material needed: construction paper, scissors, popcorn, glue, 1/4-inch red paper ribbon

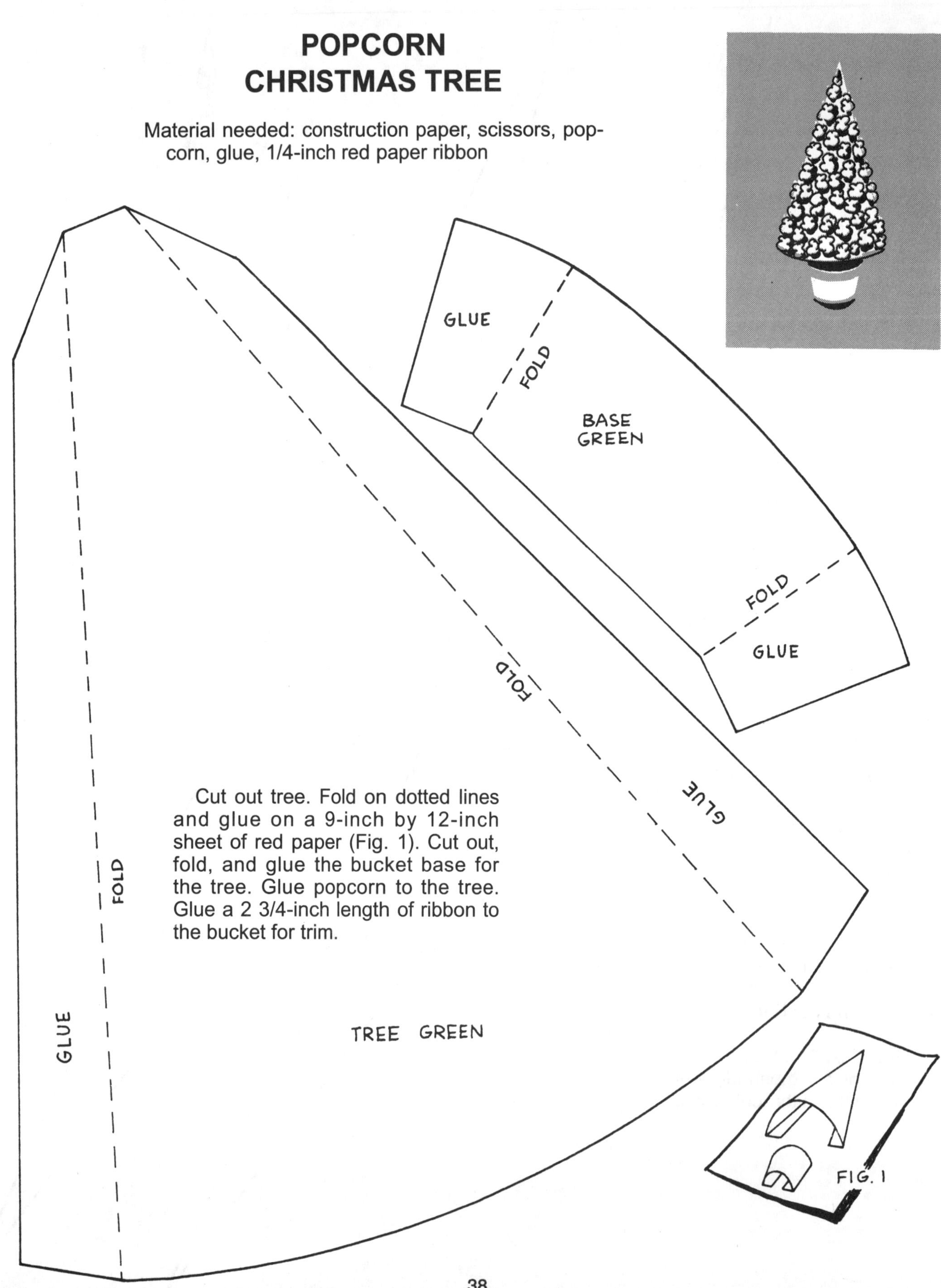

Cut out tree. Fold on dotted lines and glue on a 9-inch by 12-inch sheet of red paper (Fig. 1). Cut out, fold, and glue the bucket base for the tree. Glue popcorn to the tree. Glue a 2 3/4-inch length of ribbon to the bucket for trim.

CHERUB PLACE MAT

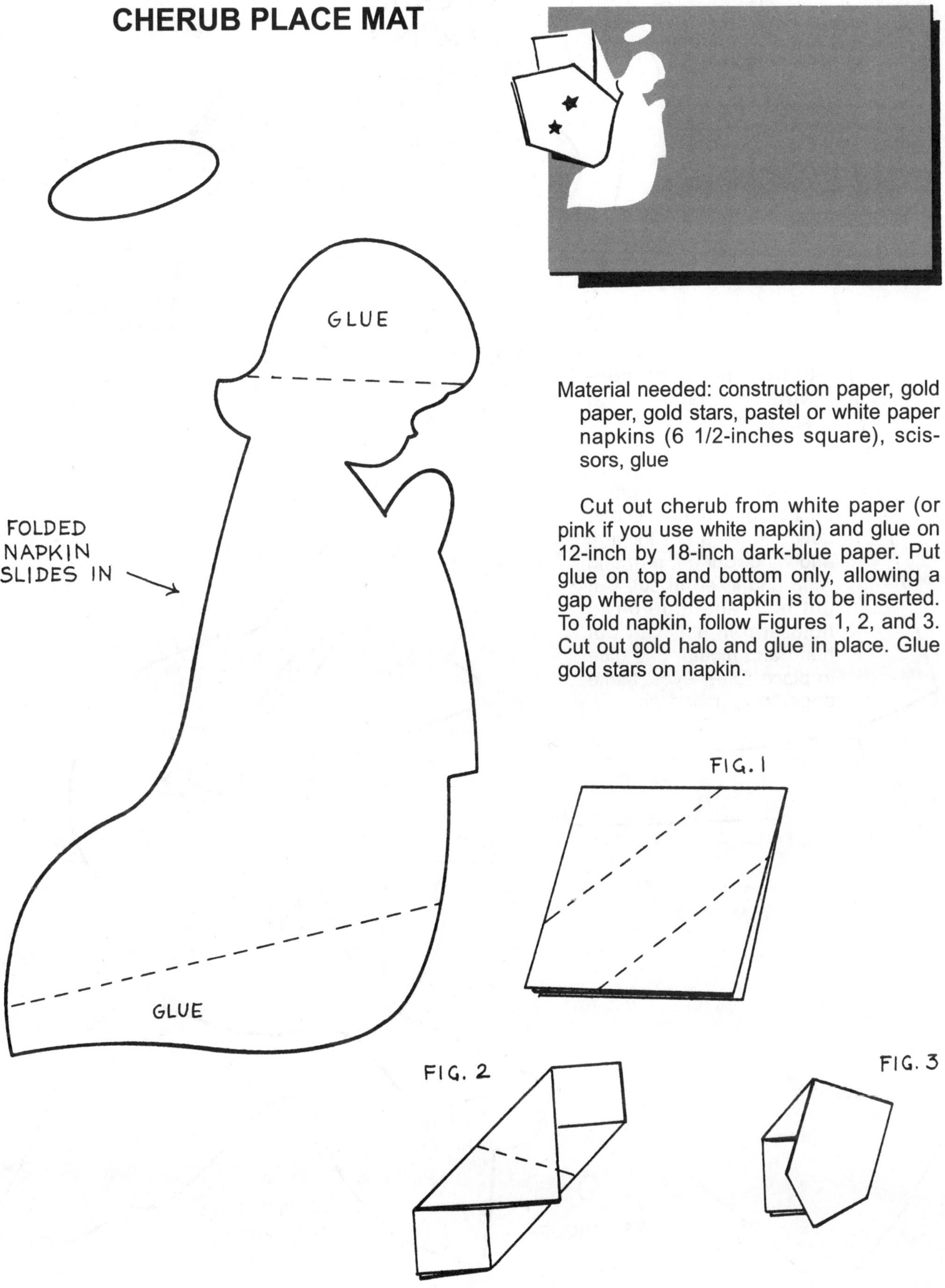

Material needed: construction paper, gold paper, gold stars, pastel or white paper napkins (6 1/2-inches square), scissors, glue

Cut out cherub from white paper (or pink if you use white napkin) and glue on 12-inch by 18-inch dark-blue paper. Put glue on top and bottom only, allowing a gap where folded napkin is to be inserted. To fold napkin, follow Figures 1, 2, and 3. Cut out gold halo and glue in place. Glue gold stars on napkin.

CHERUB PLAYING MANDOLIN

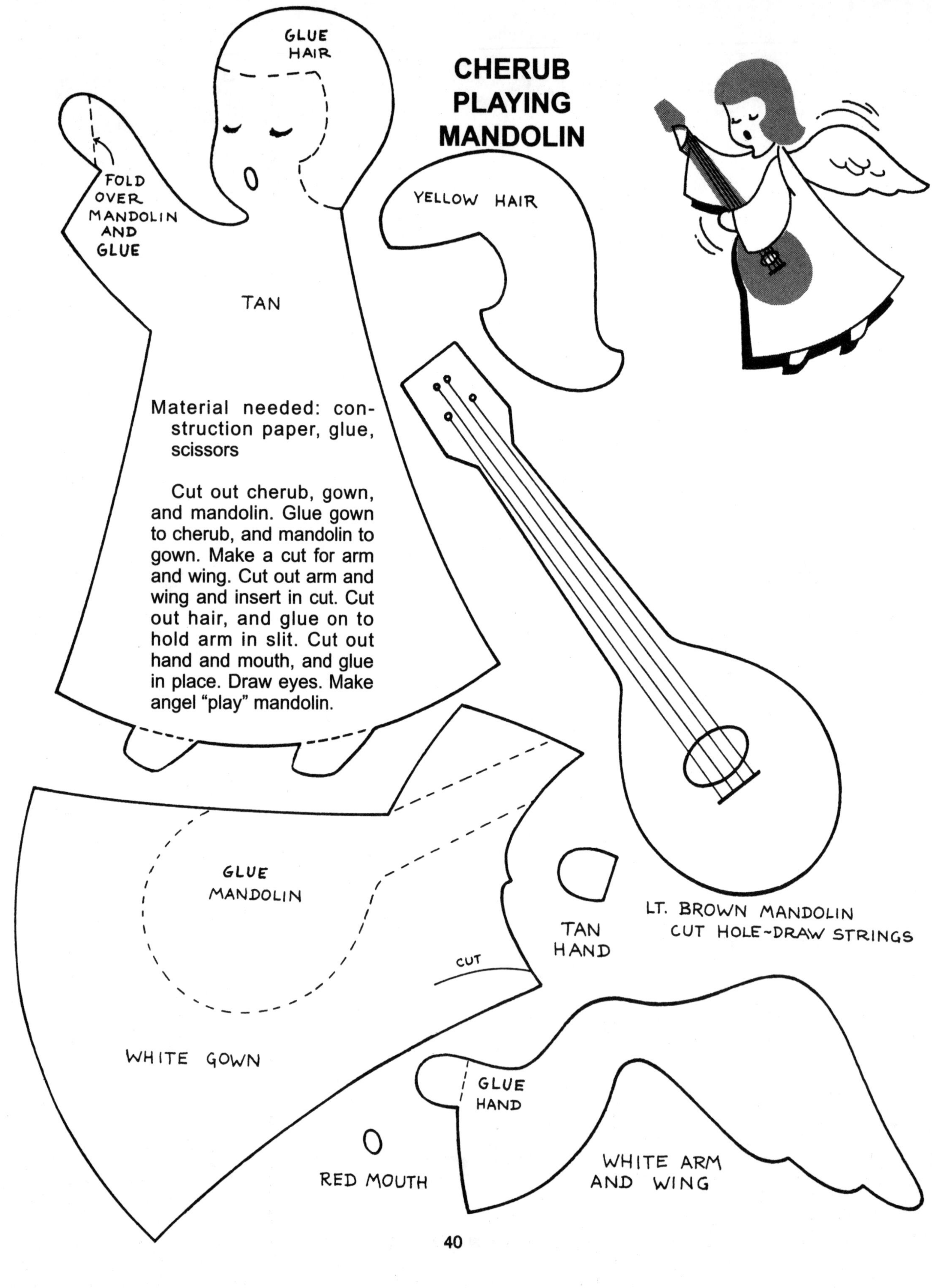

ANGEL

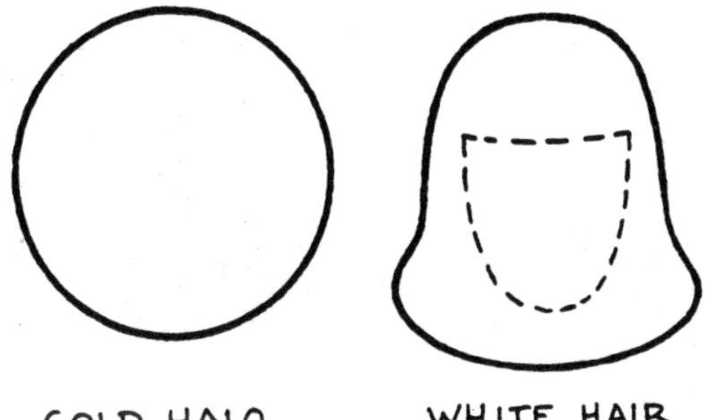

Material needed: construction paper, scissors, glue

Place wing pattern on fold of white paper, trace, and cut out. Cut out cape, and glue to wings. Cut out gown and fold accordion style on dotted lines. Glue gown to cape. Put glue on bottom of gown and clip together until dry. Add hair, face, hands, and halo as shown.

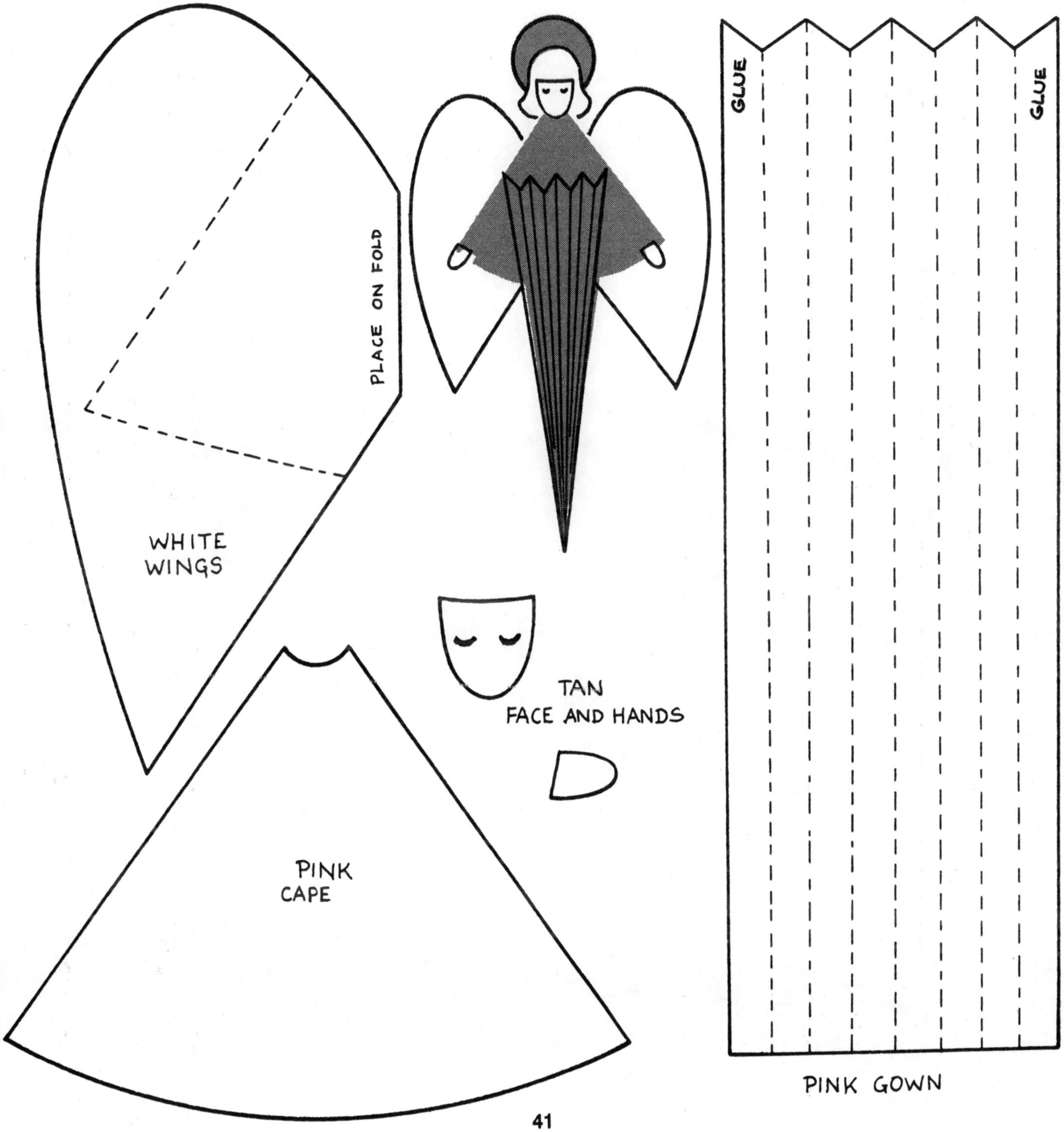

HANGING HEARTS DECORATION

Material needed: construction paper, needle and thread, ribbon, cellophane tape, scissors

Place heart patterns on fold and cut out a red and a pink heart in each size. Sew together as shown, using knots to hold the hearts in position desired. Make these in various lengths and hang in groups of threes with ribbon and cellophane tape.

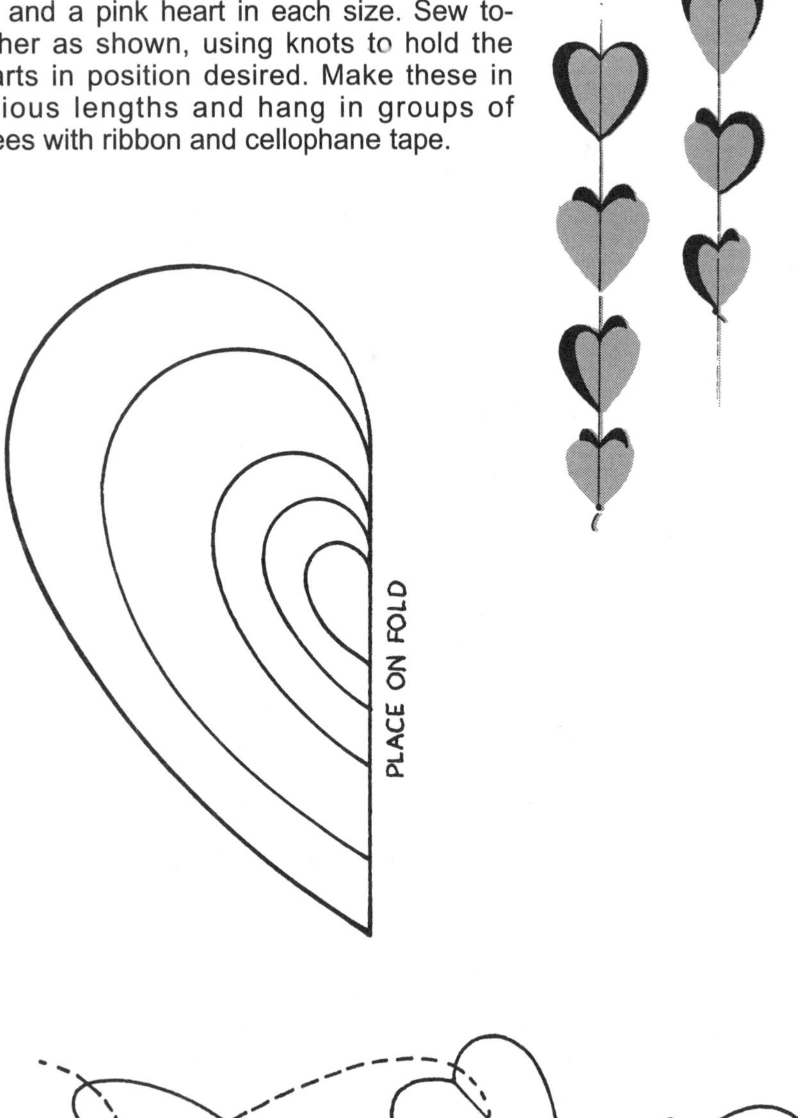

VALENTINE MAILBOX

Material needed: shoe box, scissors, construction paper, cellophane tape, glue

Cut the bottom of shoe box, rounding the sides (Fig. 2), and leaving the bottom long enough to roll over and tape (Fig. 4) on each side. Cut the lid (Fig. 1), fold flap in (Fig. 3), and tape to bottom of box. Cover box with white paper and glue pink panels down each side in front. Cut out design as indicated and decorate the box. Put a hole in the back of the box and hang on a nail. Personalize by printing child's name.

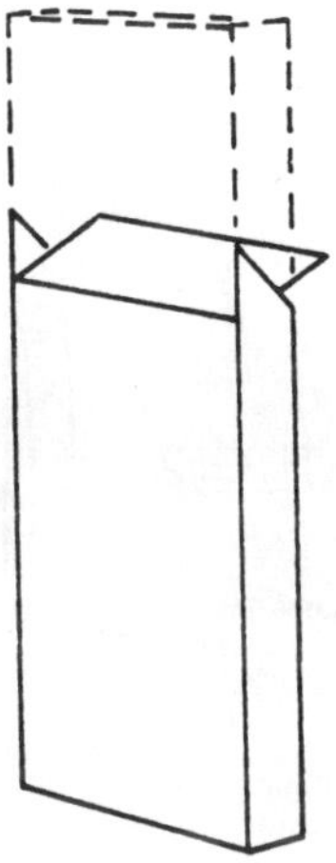

FIG. 1

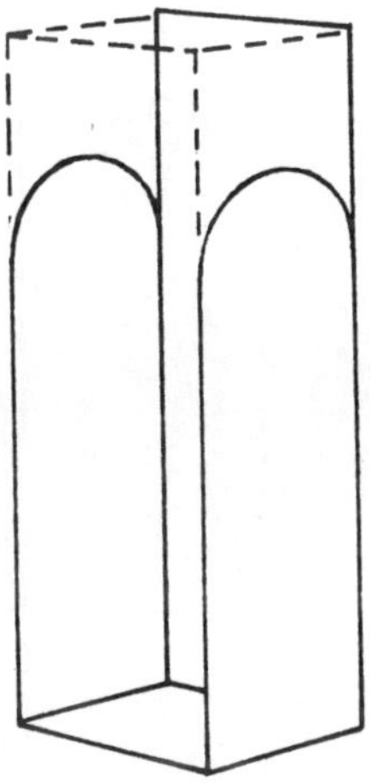

FIG. 2

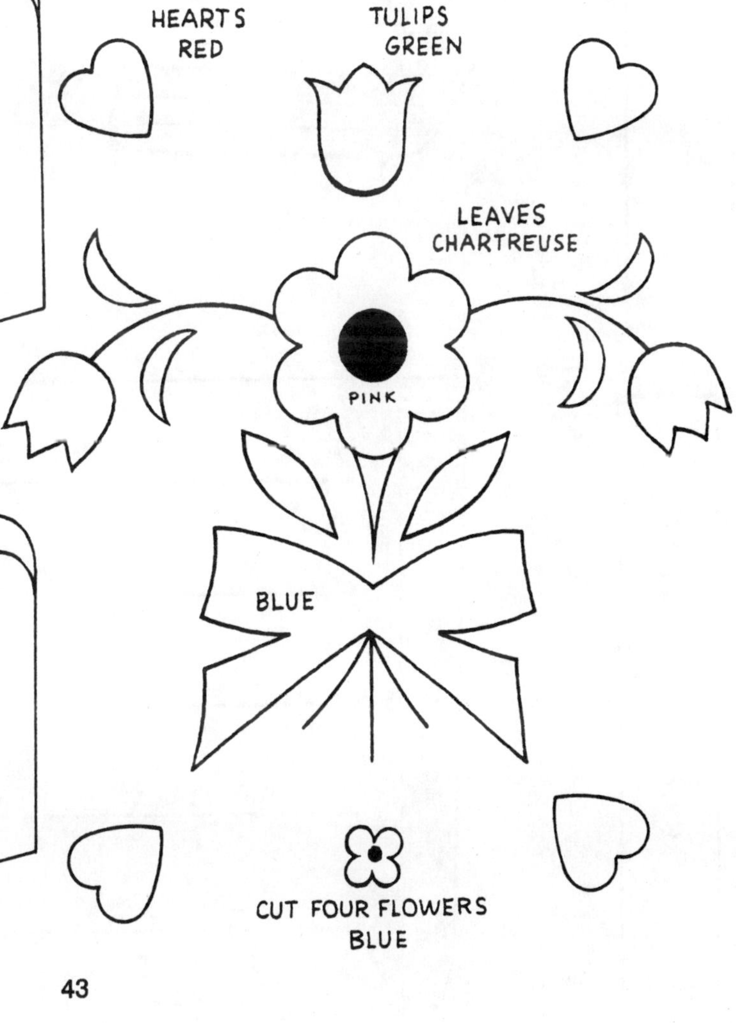

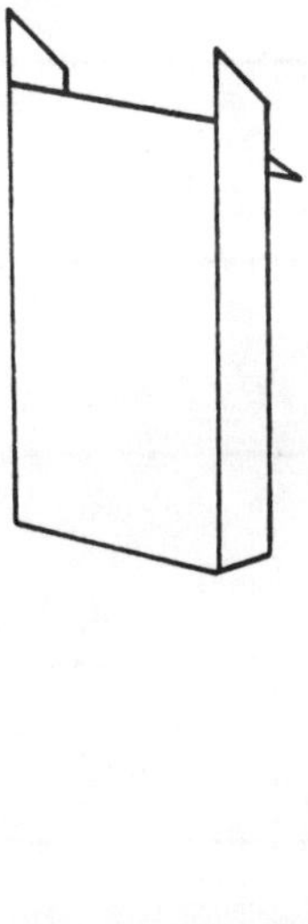

FIG. 3

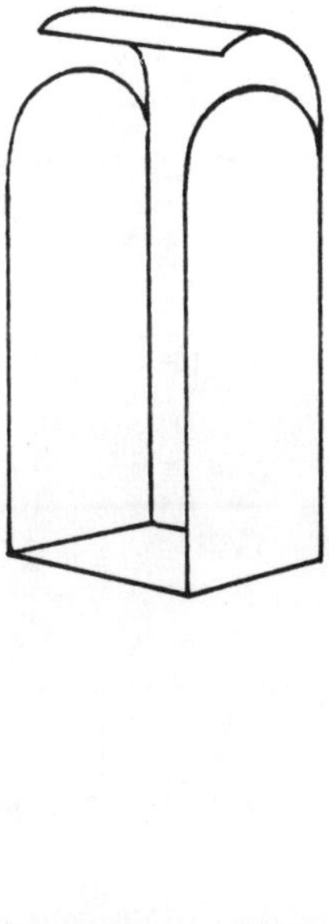

FIG. 4

HEARTS
RED

TULIPS
GREEN

LEAVES
CHARTREUSE

PINK

BLUE

CUT FOUR FLOWERS
BLUE

43

EASTER BASKET

Material needed: construction paper, scissors, glue

Place basket pattern on fold of paper and cut out. Fold basket and cut slits (Fig. 1). Glue ends of basket and handle (Fig. 2). Cut out fourteen 3 1/16-inch by 1/2-inch strips of paper—four blue, four yellow-green, four purple, and two white. Weave strips in and out through the slits (Fig. 3), alternating colors. Cut two 6-inch by 1/2-inch strips and glue on rim of basket (Fig. 2). Glue down bottom of strips.

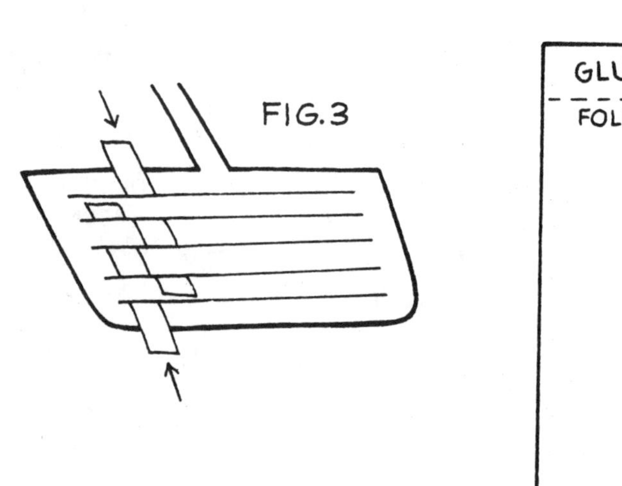

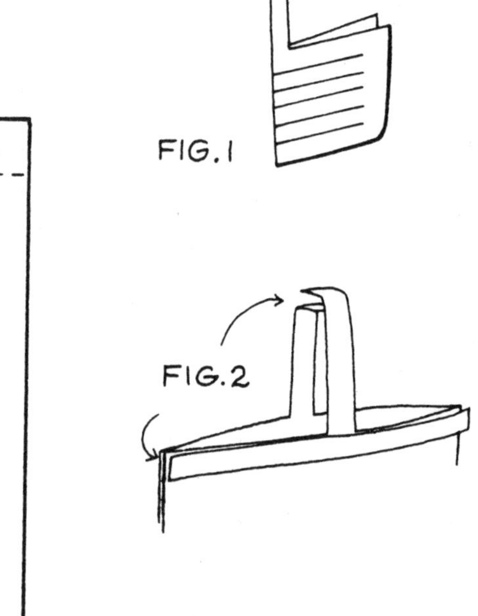

CORNUCOPIA

Material needed: construction paper, tissue paper (brown, yellow, and orange variegated), scissors, glue

Place cornucopia pattern on fold of paper and cut out. Cut slits as indicated. Roll and glue ends together (Fig. 1). Cut out large leaf from a full sheet of construction paper (see Fig. 1 for shape of leaf). Accordion fold variegated tissue paper (Fig. 2). Place small leaf pattern on fold and cut out ten leaves.

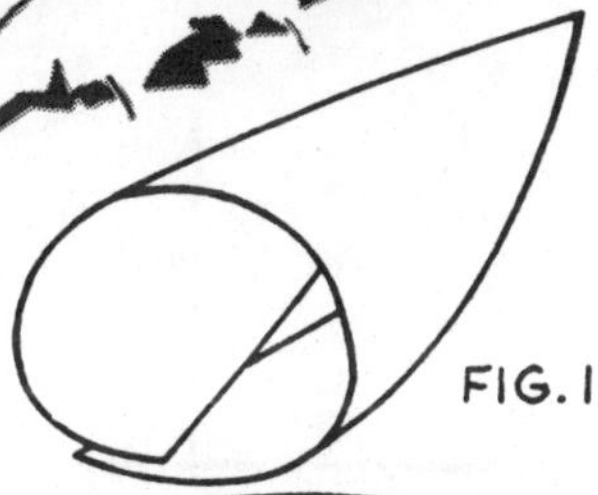

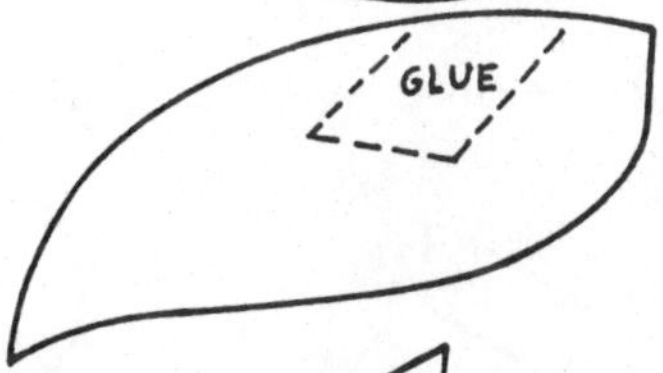

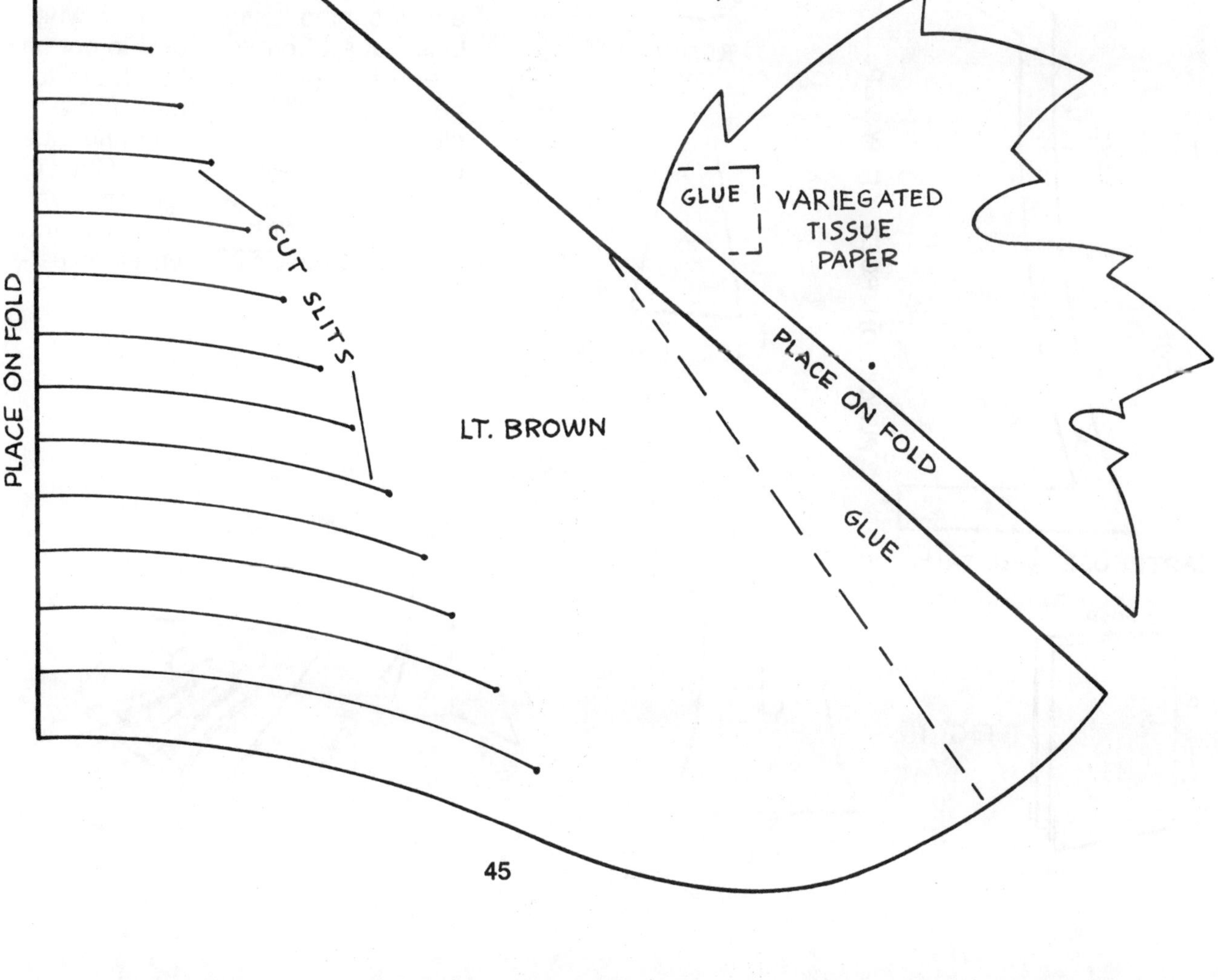

BELL CARD

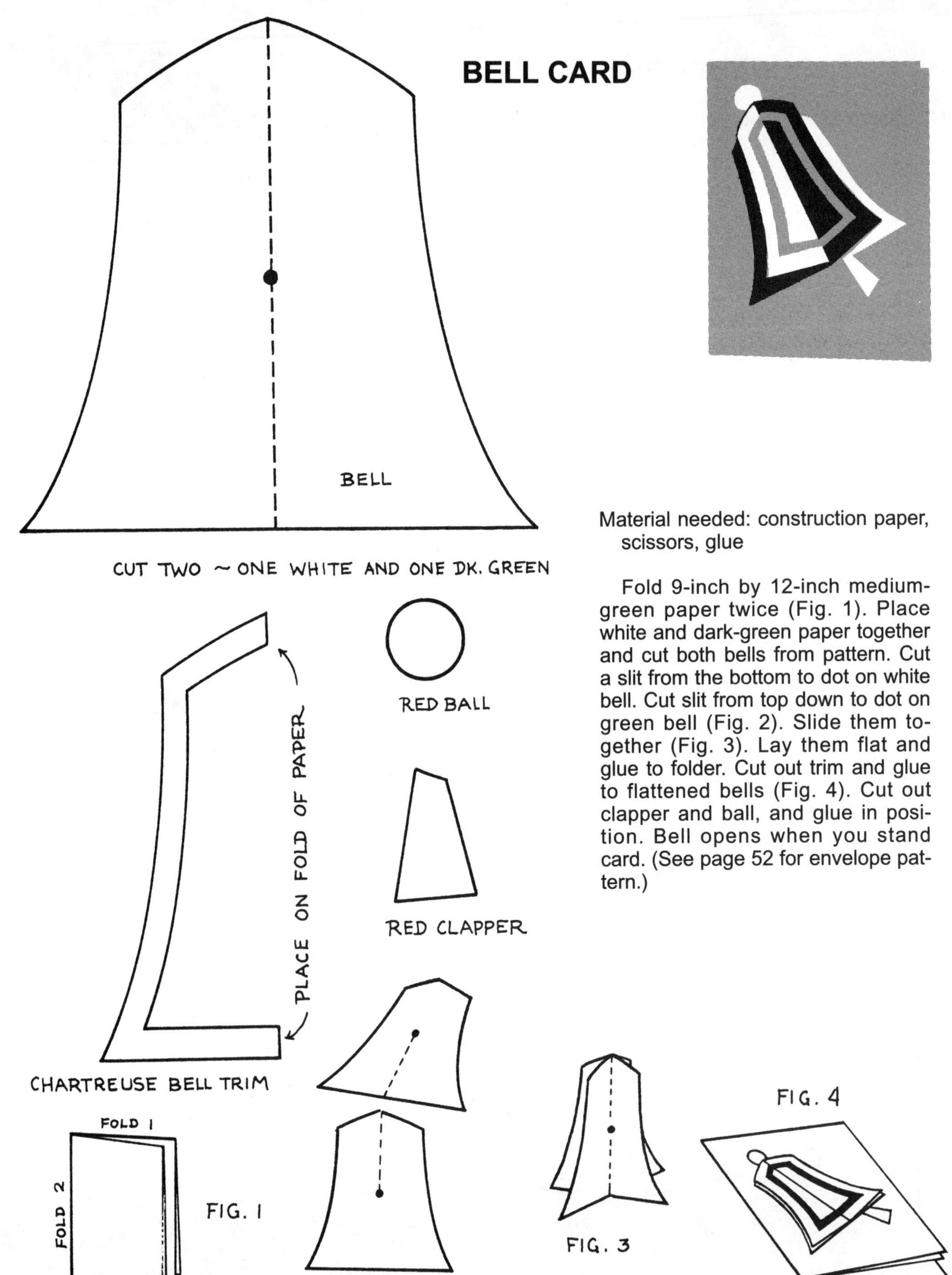

Material needed: construction paper, scissors, glue

Fold 9-inch by 12-inch medium-green paper twice (Fig. 1). Place white and dark-green paper together and cut both bells from pattern. Cut a slit from the bottom to dot on white bell. Cut slit from top down to dot on green bell (Fig. 2). Slide them together (Fig. 3). Lay them flat and glue to folder. Cut out trim and glue to flattened bells (Fig. 4). Cut out clapper and ball, and glue in position. Bell opens when you stand card. (See page 52 for envelope pattern.)

BETHLEHEM CARD

Material needed: construction paper, scissors, glue

Fold 9-inch by 12-inch dark-blue paper twice (Fig. 1). Fold purple paper in half, place scene pattern on fold, and cut out. Cut out hills and glue on bottom of folder. Glue scene onto hills. Cut out strips and glue on to form star. (See page 52 for envelope pattern.)

FIG. 1

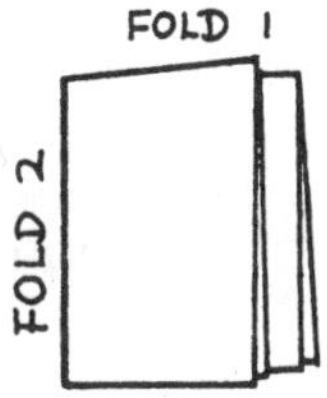

FOLD 1

FOLD 2

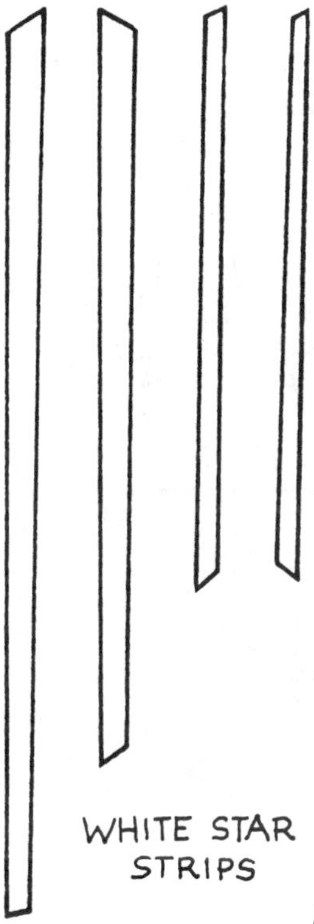

WHITE STAR STRIPS

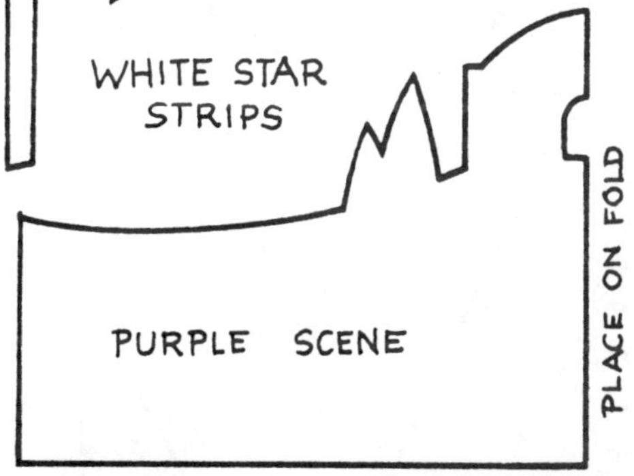

PURPLE SCENE

PLACE ON FOLD

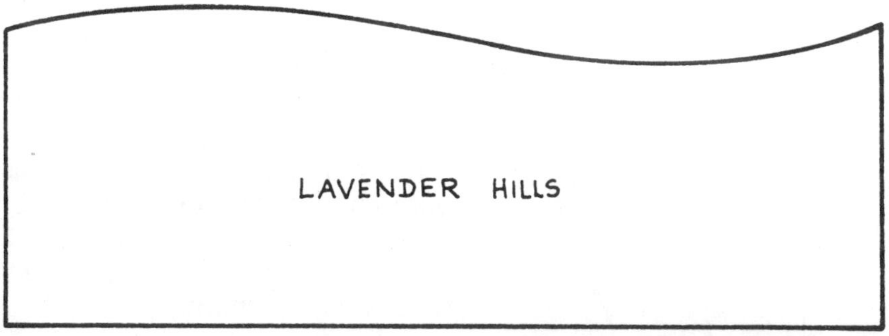

LAVENDER HILLS

KINGS AND SHEPHERD CARD

Material needed: construction paper, scissors, glue

Fold 9-inch by 12-inch purple paper twice (Fig. 1). Cut staff and glue to folder. Cut three crowns and glue to folder as shown. Decorate with trims and diamonds. (See page 52 for envelope pattern.)

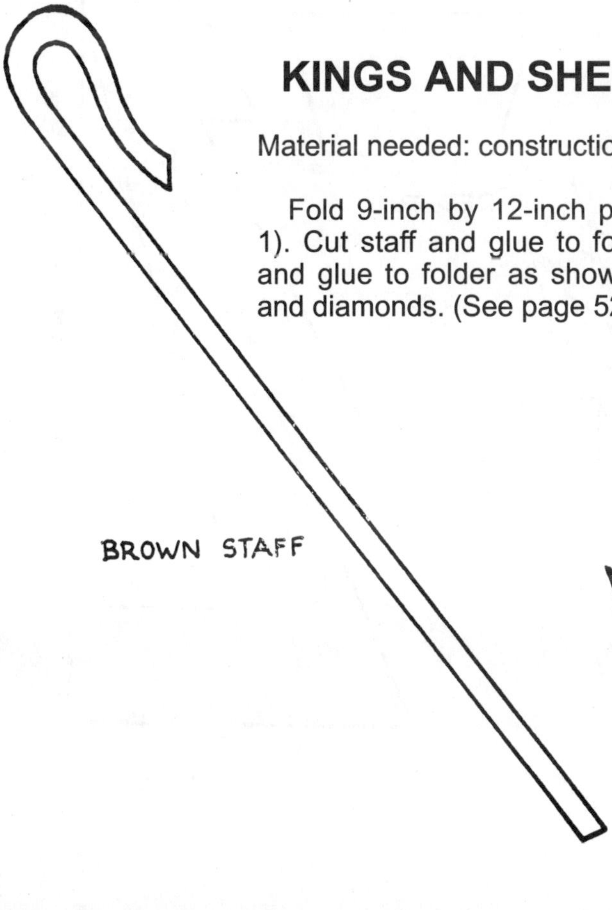

BROWN STAFF

FIG. 1

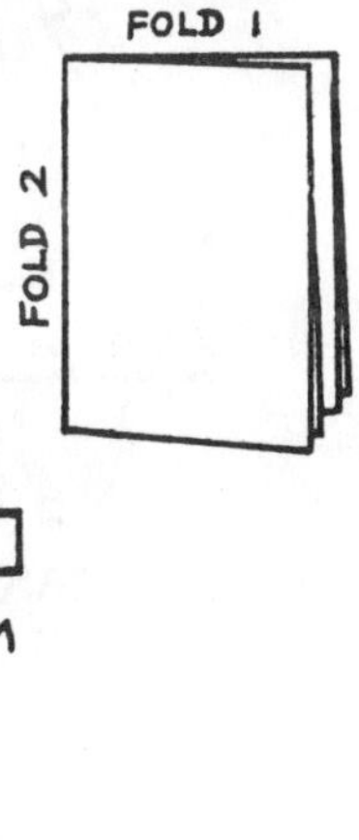

FOLD 1

FOLD 2

YELLOW CROWN

RED DIAMOND

ORANGE TRIM

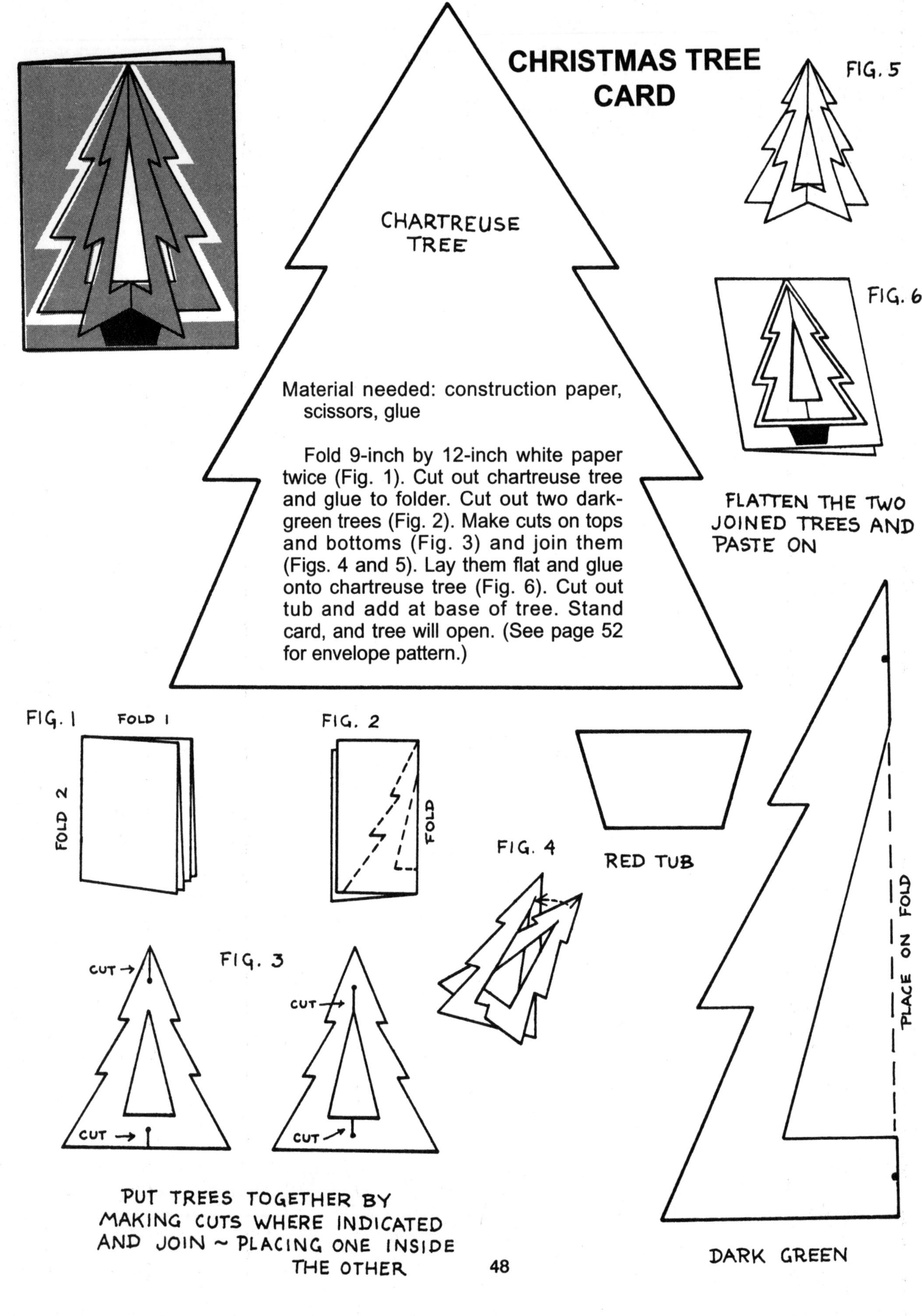

CHRISTMAS TREE CARD
FIG. 5
FIG. 6
CHARTREUSE TREE
Material needed: construction paper, scissors, glue

Fold 9-inch by 12-inch white paper twice (Fig. 1). Cut out chartreuse tree and glue to folder. Cut out two dark-green trees (Fig. 2). Make cuts on tops and bottoms (Fig. 3) and join them (Figs. 4 and 5). Lay them flat and glue onto chartreuse tree (Fig. 6). Cut out tub and add at base of tree. Stand card, and tree will open. (See page 52 for envelope pattern.)

FLATTEN THE TWO JOINED TREES AND PASTE ON

FIG. 1
FOLD 1
FOLD 2
FIG. 2
FOLD
FIG. 4
RED TUB
FIG. 3
CUT →
CUT →
CUT →
CUT →
PLACE ON FOLD
PUT TREES TOGETHER BY MAKING CUTS WHERE INDICATED AND JOIN ~ PLACING ONE INSIDE THE OTHER
DARK GREEN

EASTER CARD

Material needed: construction paper, lavender
   tissue paper, scissors, glue

   Fold 9-inch by 12-inch white paper twice (Figs. 1
and 2). Cut out the church window from the first two
pages. Glue a 3-inch by 5-inch sheet of lavender
tissue paper between the first and second pages.
Cut out and glue cross, lilies, and stem. (See page
52 for envelope pattern.)

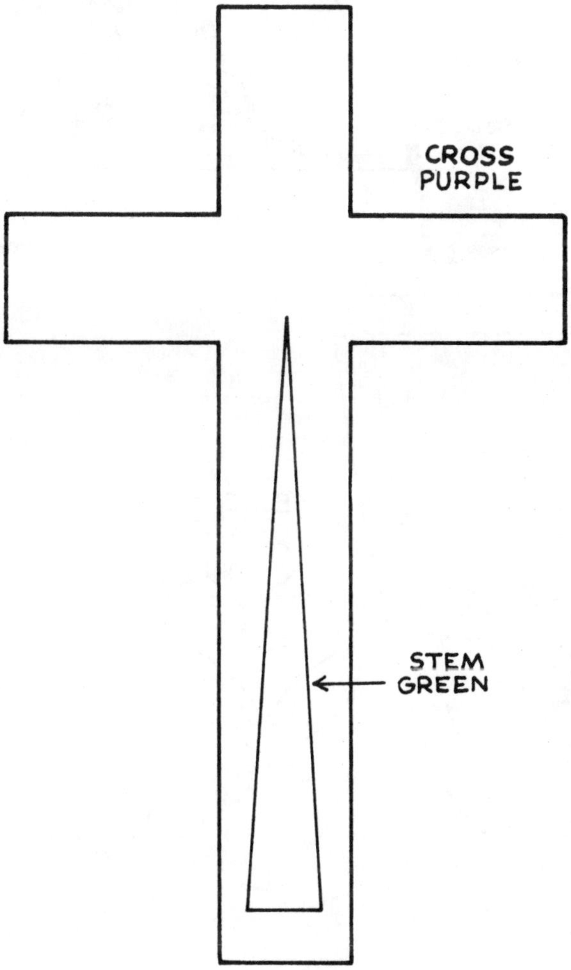

CROSS
PURPLE

STEM
GREEN

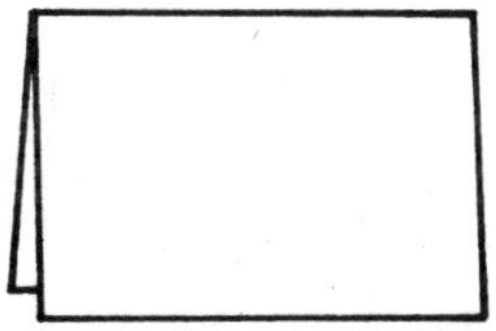

FIG. 1

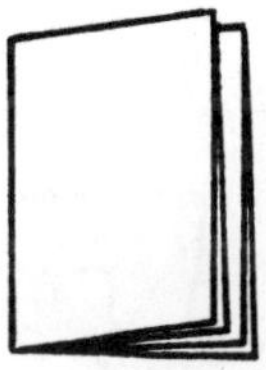

FIG. 2

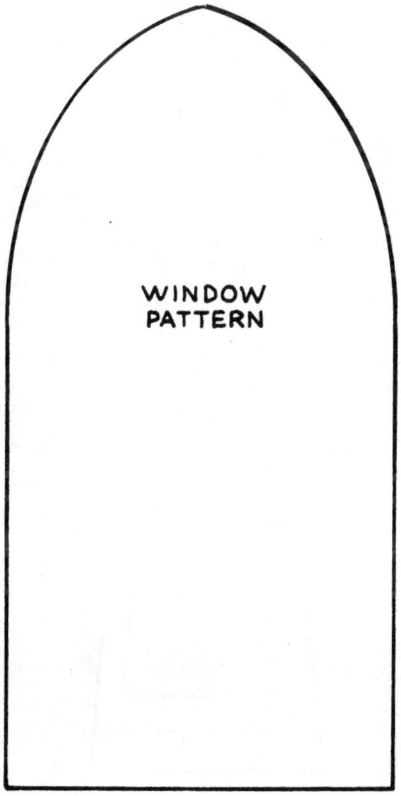

WINDOW
PATTERN

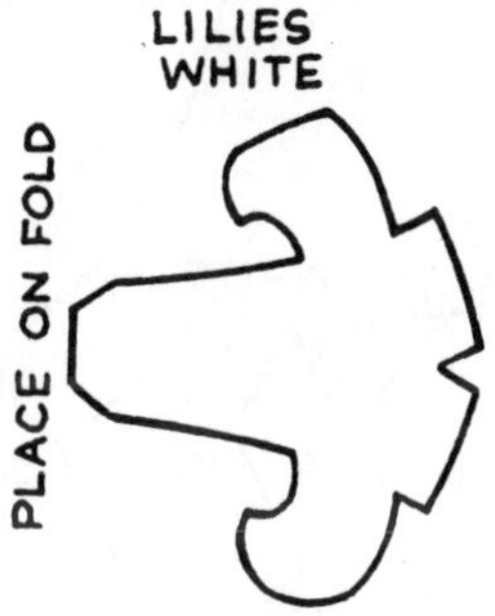

LILIES
WHITE

PLACE ON FOLD

MOTHER'S DAY CARD

Material needed: construction paper, scissors, glue

Cut out A of light-blue, B and C of white paper. Glue together as in Fig. 1. (Glue only the lower part of C so that a 2 1/4-inch by 1 3/4-inch card can be inserted as shown.) Cut out decorations and glue as indicated. Draw lines with black crayon or felt-tip marker. (See page 52 for envelope pattern.)

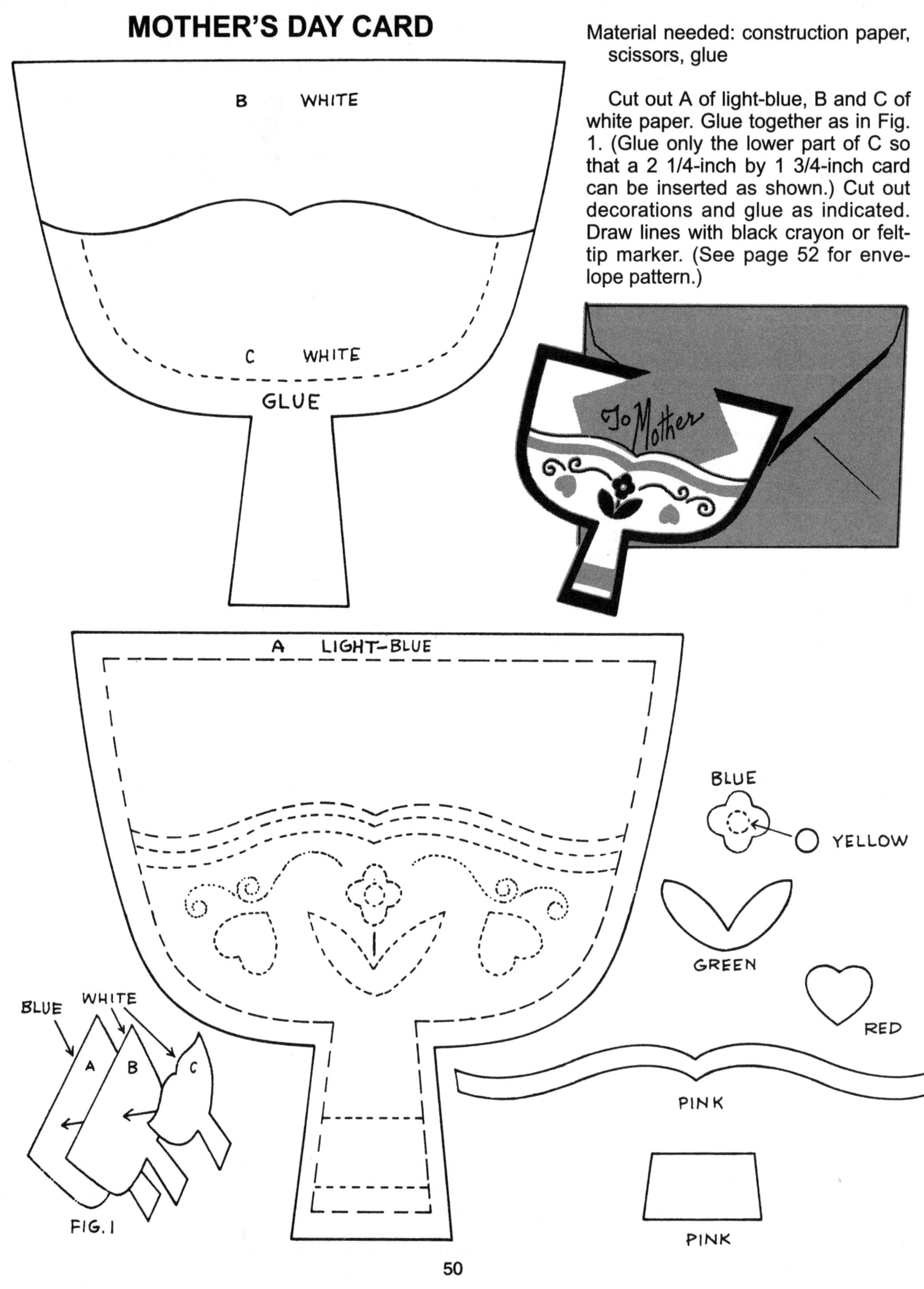

FATHER'S DAY CARD

Material needed: construction paper, scissors, glue

Fold 9-inch by 12-inch white paper twice (Figs. 1 and 2). Cut out filing cabinet. Glue on front of card. Cut out panel and handles and glue on cabinet. Now open folded card (Fig. 3) and cut slit. Cut out yellow strip and write message as shown. Insert this strip into slit, leaving part showing to pull out. (See page 52 for envelope pattern.)

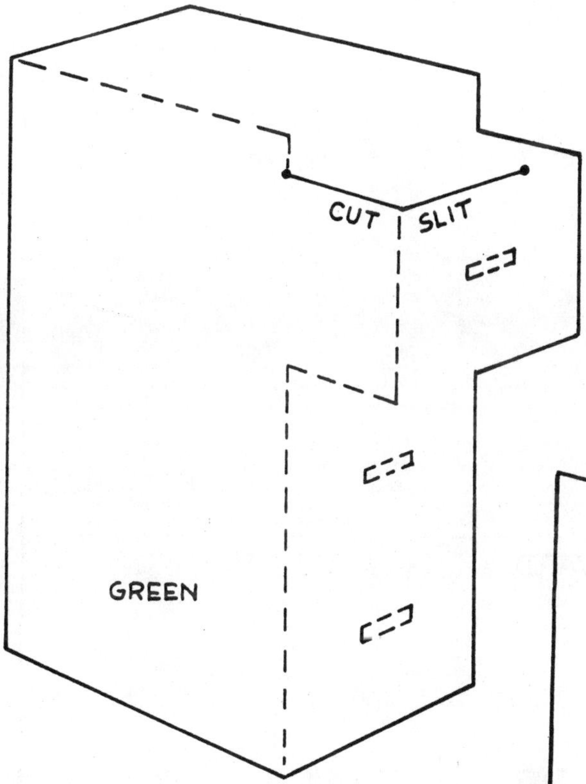

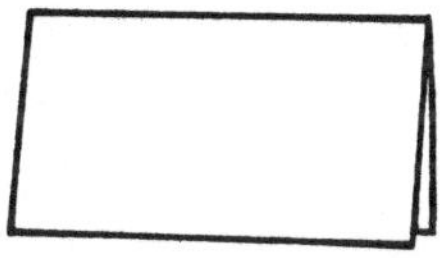

FIG. I

FIG. 2

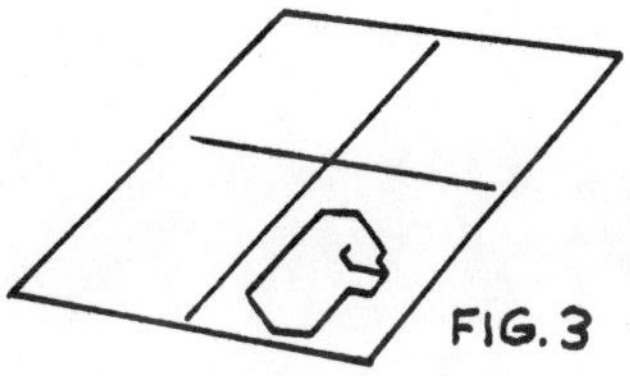

FIG. 3

CUT SLIT

GREEN

HANDLES   BLACK

DK. GREEN

YOU'RE TOP DRAWER WITH ME!

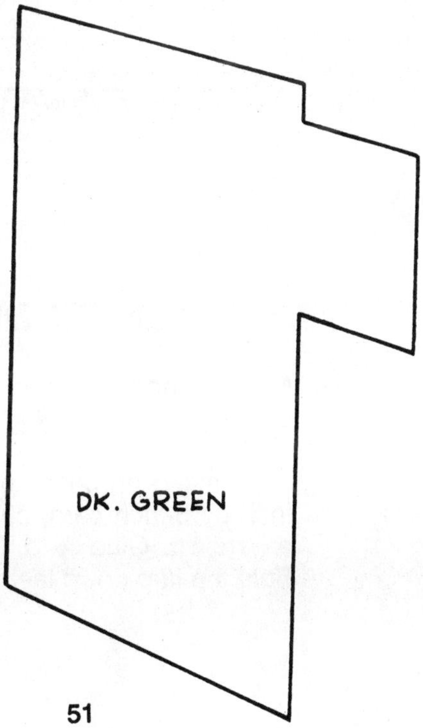

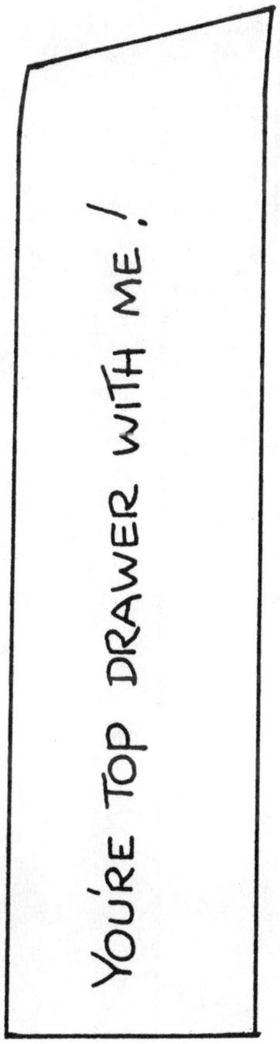

YELLOW

FOLD FORWARD

FOLD FORWARD

FOLD FORWARD

GLUE B

GLUE A

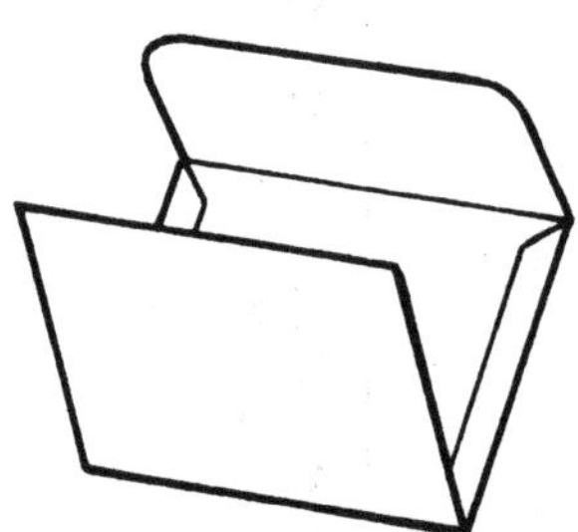

FOLD FORWARD

B

A

ENVELOPE

Material needed: glue, construction
paper, scissors

To make an envelope for a 4 1/2-
inch by 6-inch card, cut out and fold
as shown. Glue A to A and B to B.
Fold top flap down last.

FLAP 1

GRANNY RECIPE BOX

Material needed: recipe box, self-adhesive plastic, construction paper, lace paper doily, scissors, glue

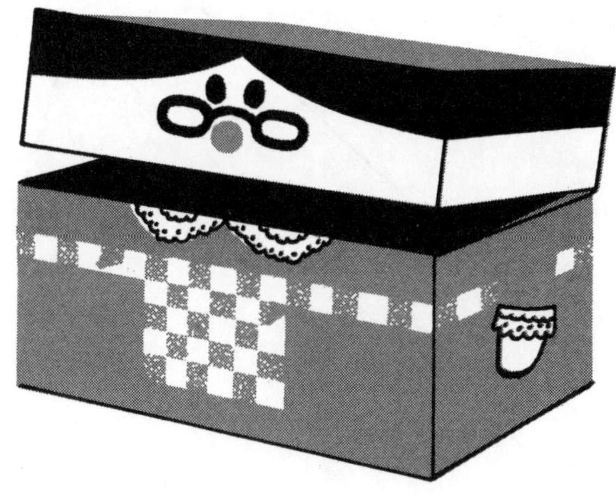

Place face pattern on fold of pink self-adhesive plastic and cut out. Stick to front and sides of box top. Cut out hair of black self-adhesive plastic and stick over pink along top edge of lid as shown. Cut apron of red and white checkered self-adhesive plastic and stick around front and sides of bottom of box—make cuts on dotted lines to indicate sleeves. Cut out pink hands and stick on where sleeve ends. Cut out collar and cuffs from doily and glue as shown. Cut out nose, eyes, and glasses from construction paper and glue on.

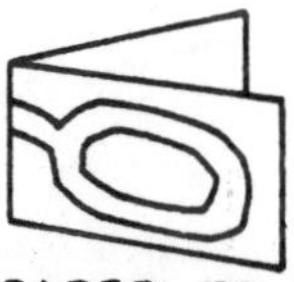

FOLD PAPER TO
CUT GLASSES

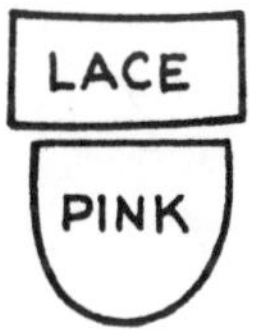

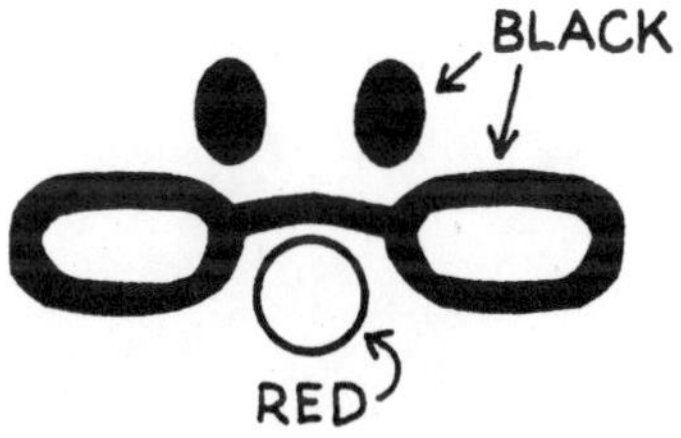

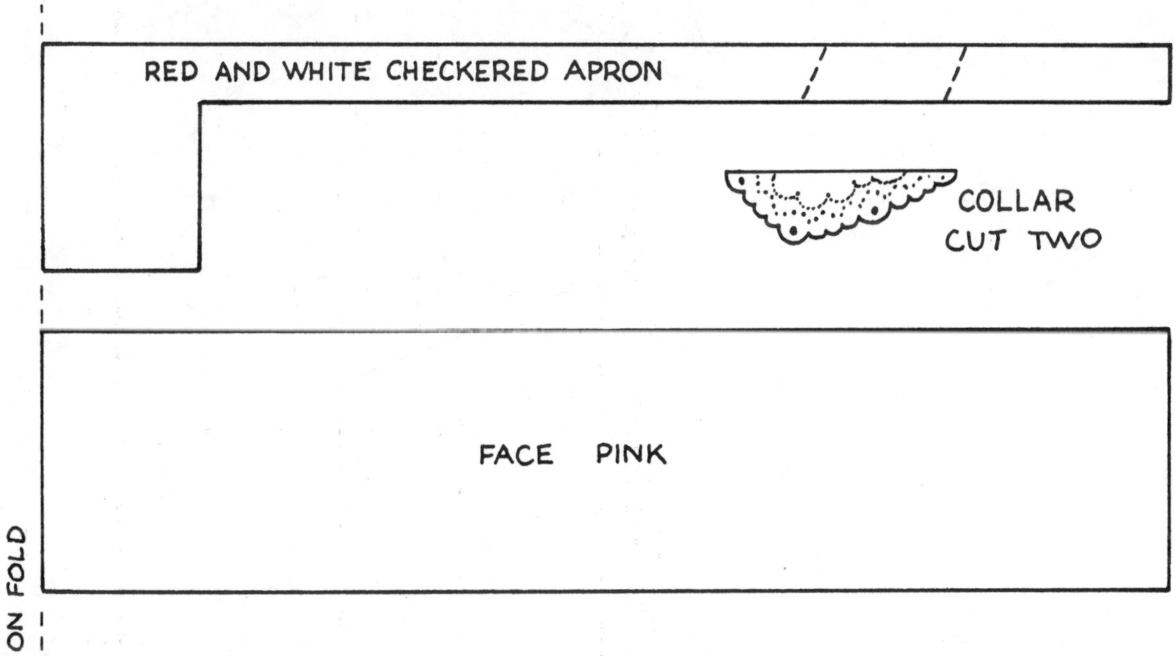

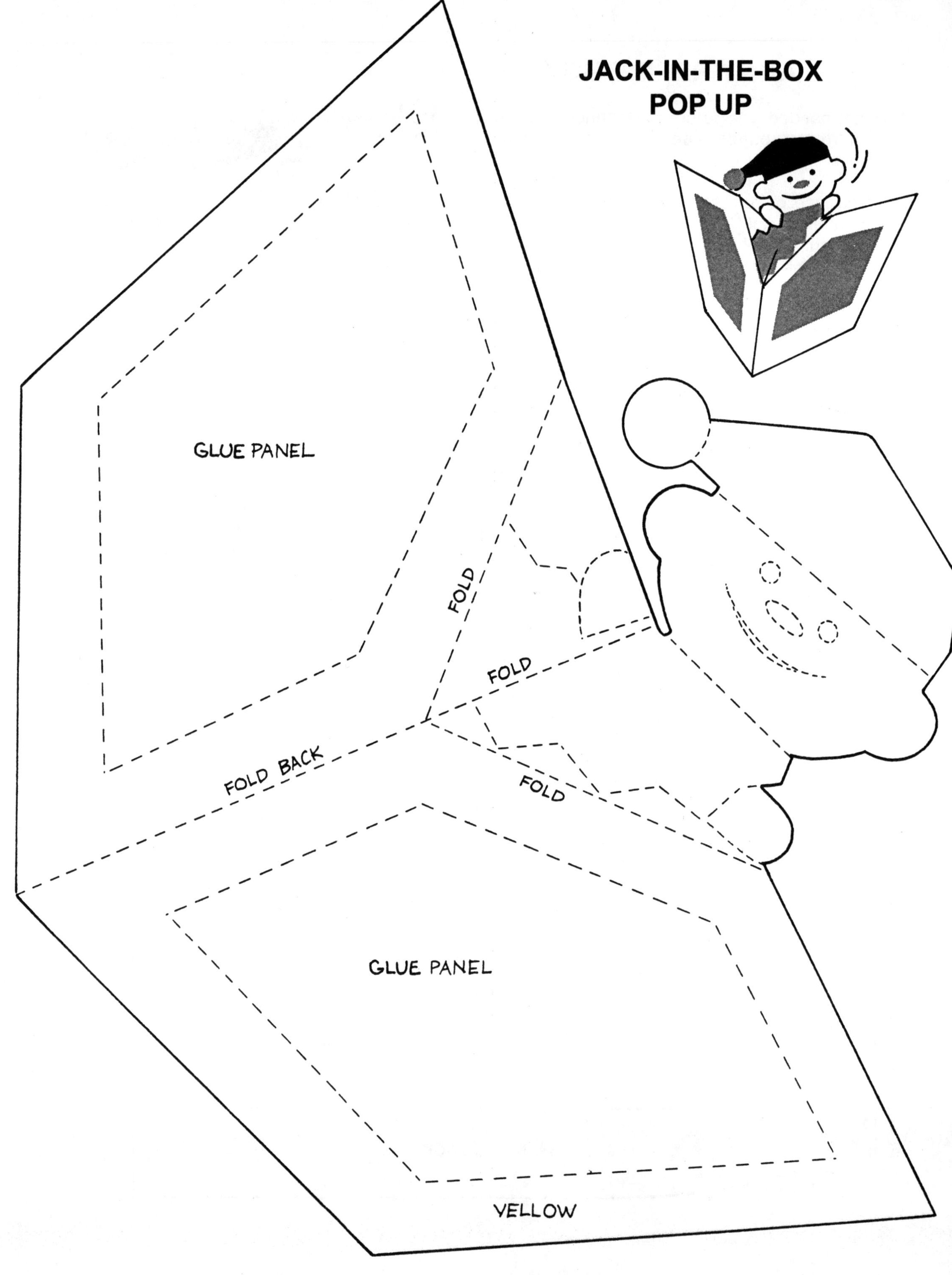

JACK-IN-THE-BOX
POP UP
GLUE PANEL
FOLD
FOLD
FOLD BACK
FOLD
GLUE PANEL
YELLOW

Material needed: construction paper, scissors, glue

Cut out box with pop-up figure and fold as shown (Fig. 1). The head will fold inside (Fig. 2). Cut out and glue panels, body, face, hands, nose, and ball. Draw eyes and mouth. Fold box and open for animation.

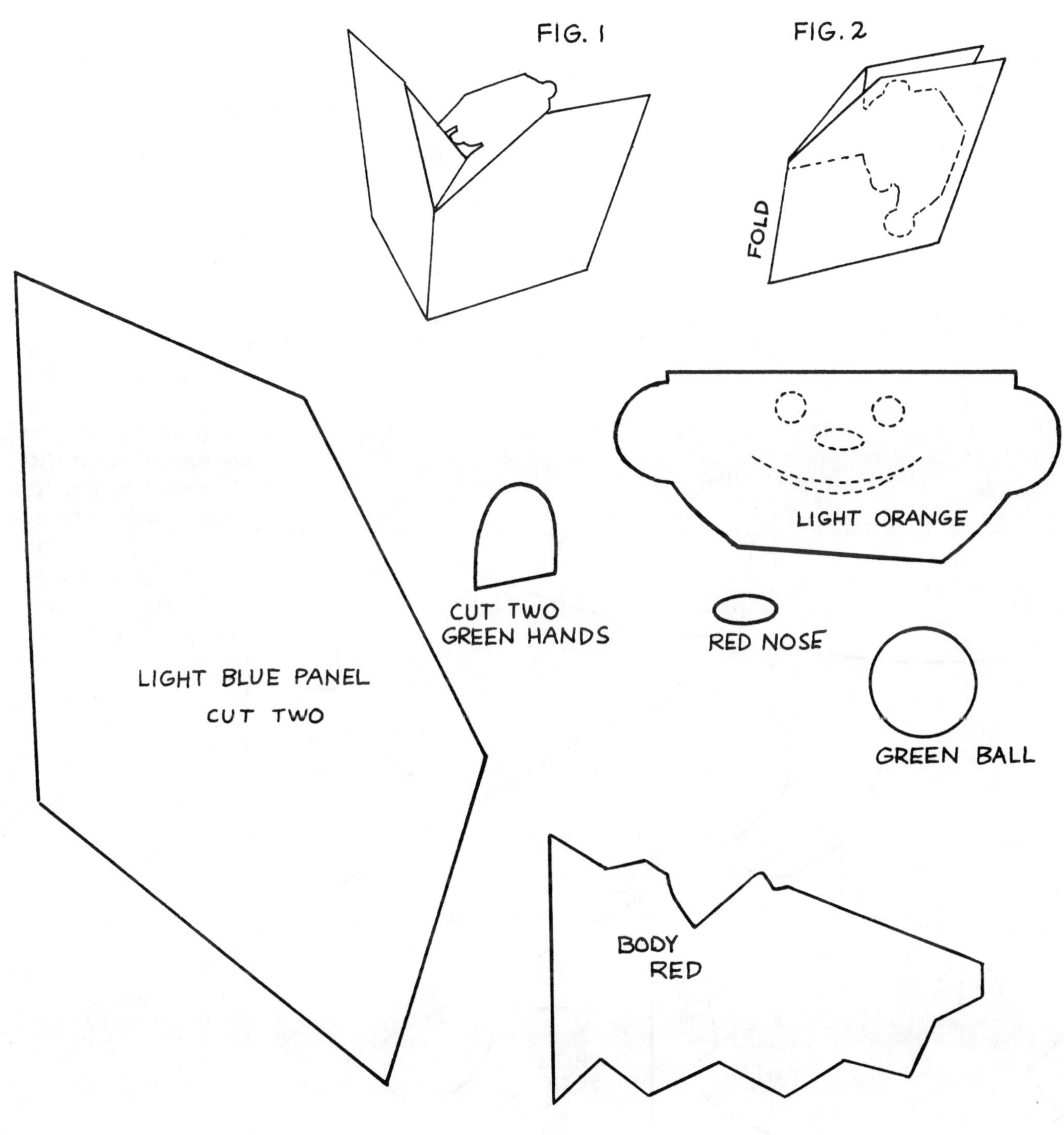

GIRL DOLL

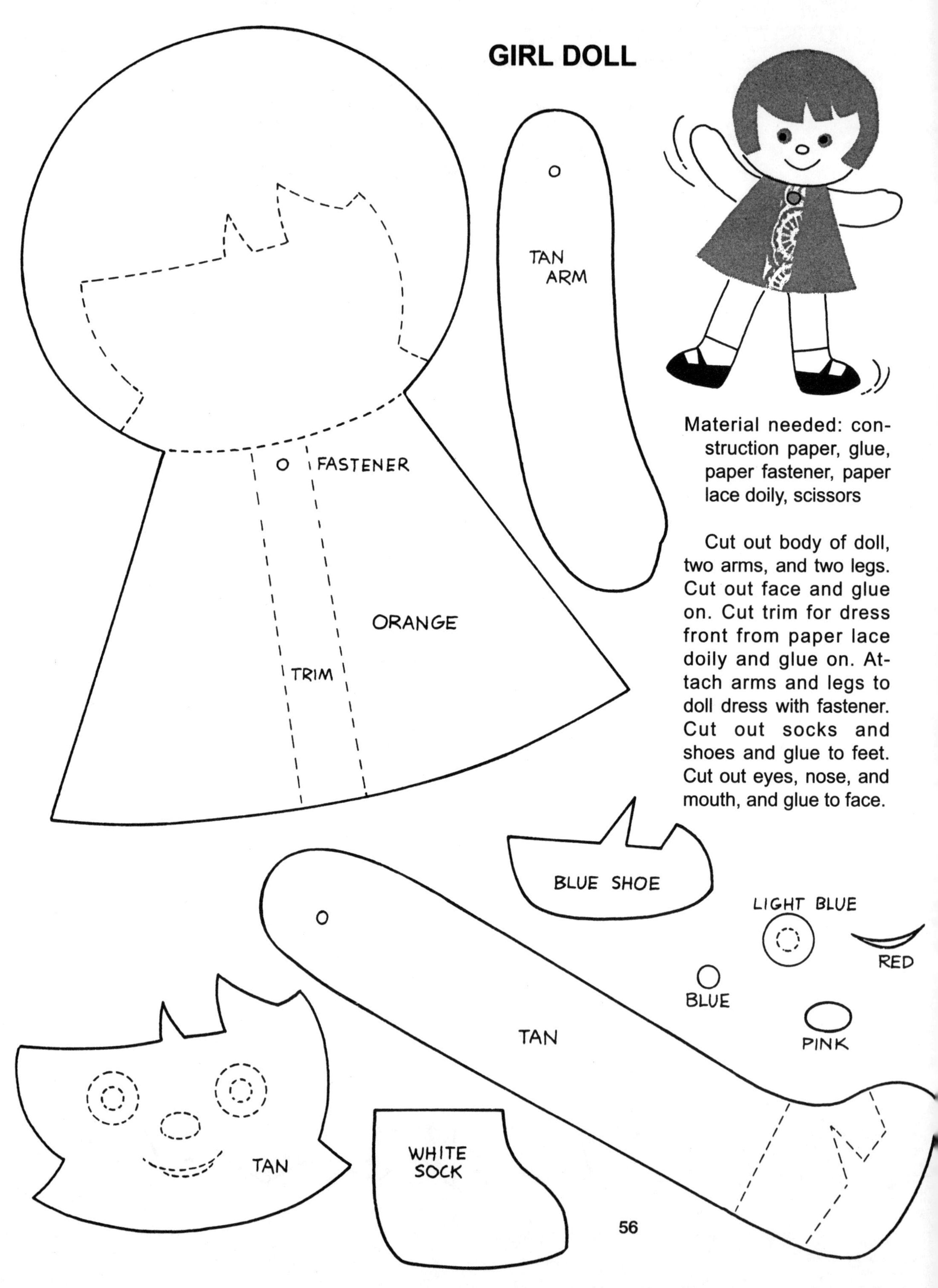

Material needed: construction paper, glue, paper fastener, paper lace doily, scissors

Cut out body of doll, two arms, and two legs. Cut out face and glue on. Cut trim for dress front from paper lace doily and glue on. Attach arms and legs to doll dress with fastener. Cut out socks and shoes and glue to feet. Cut out eyes, nose, and mouth, and glue to face.

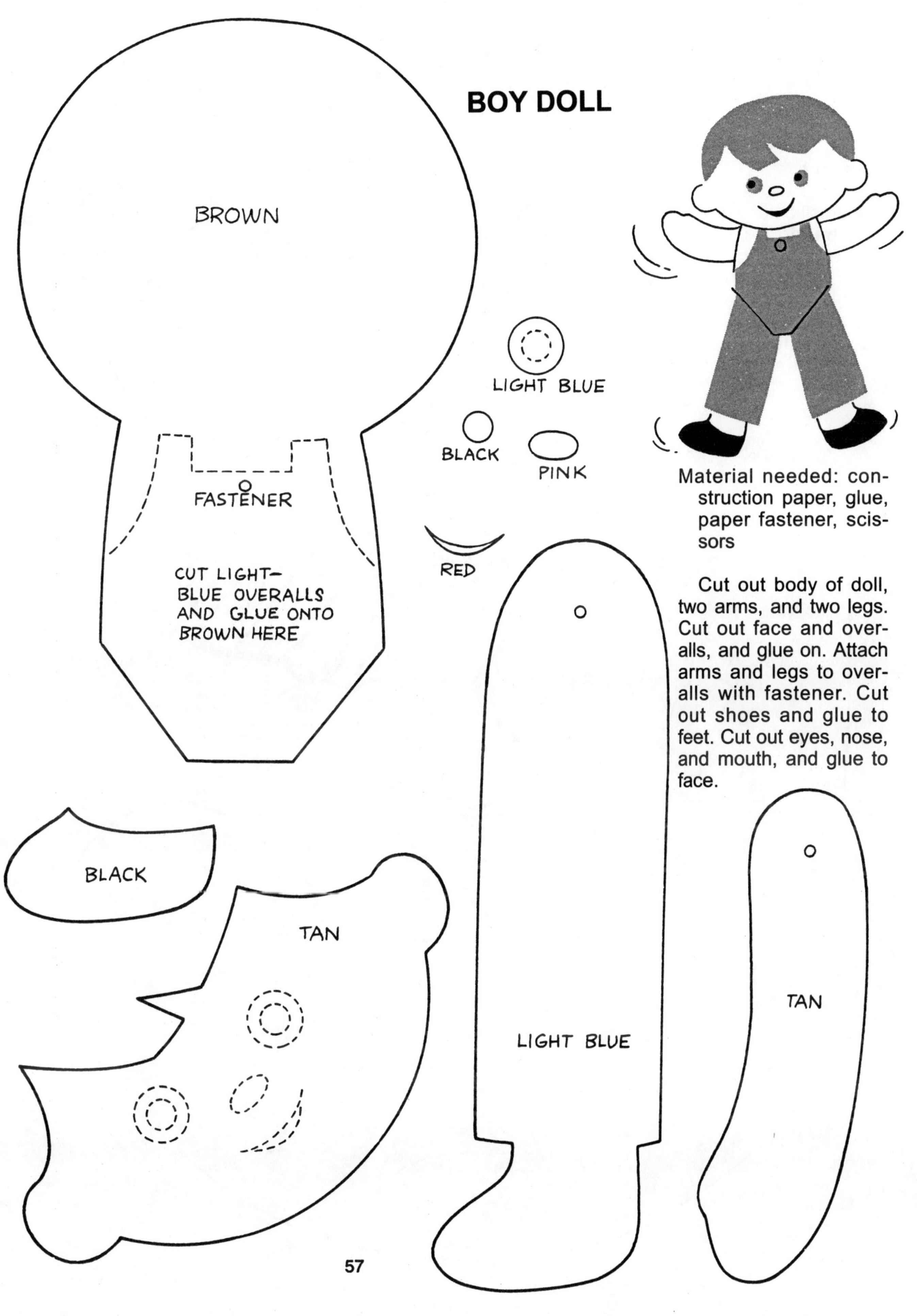

BOY DOLL

Material needed: construction paper, glue, paper fastener, scissors

Cut out body of doll, two arms, and two legs. Cut out face and overalls, and glue on. Attach arms and legs to overalls with fastener. Cut out shoes and glue to feet. Cut out eyes, nose, and mouth, and glue to face.

BALLOON BIRTHDAY CLOWN

Material needed: long balloon, 12-inch paper plate, construction paper, orange crepe paper, scissors, glue

Cut small hole in center of plate to insert balloon. Cut out lips and mouth and glue to bottom of plate. Cut out two eyebrows and two eyes and glue on. Fold a piece of crepe paper as in Fig. 1. Fringe and cut in two to make hair. Glue one on each side, doubling over the edge of plate.

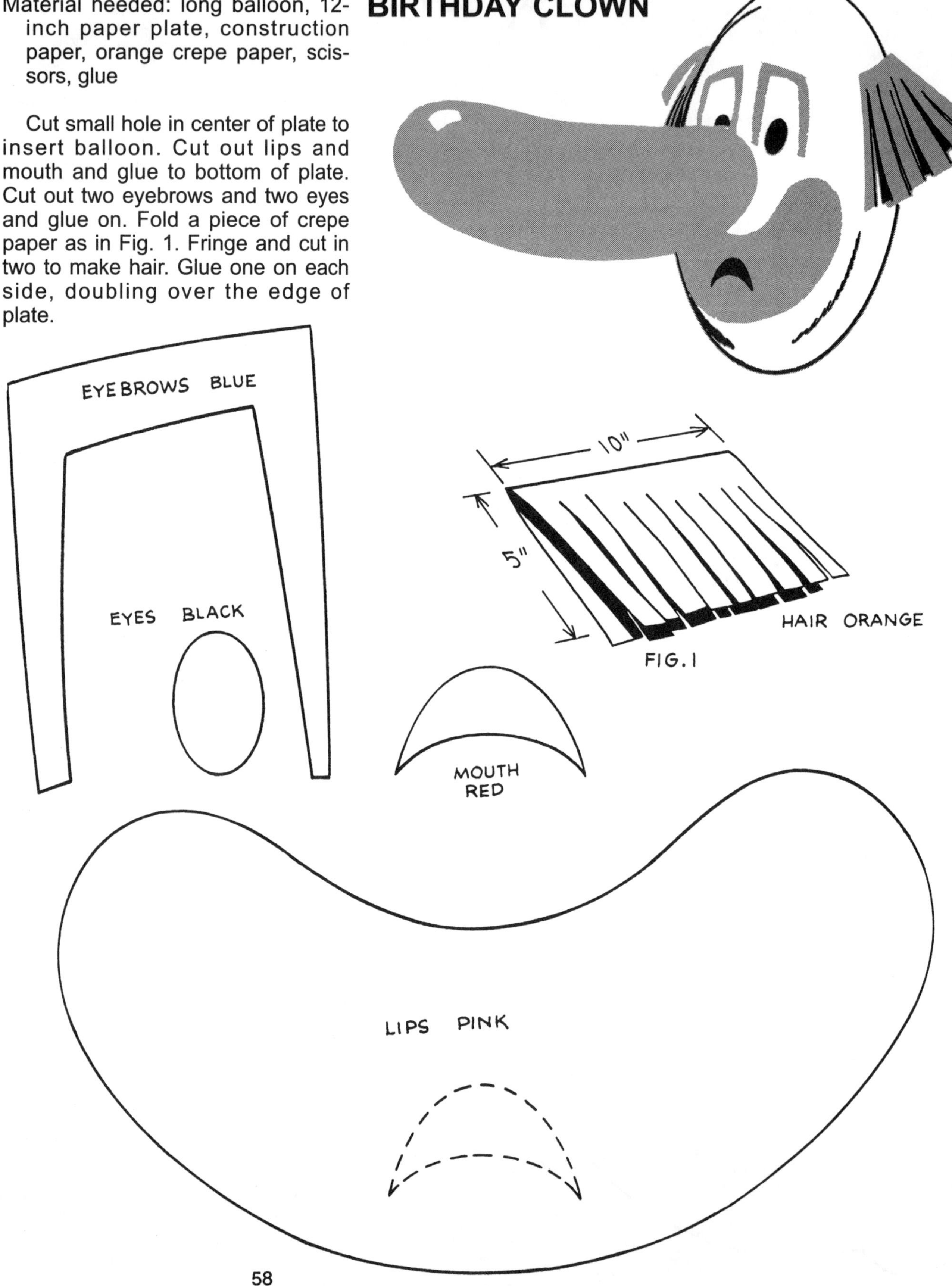

ROCKING HORSE

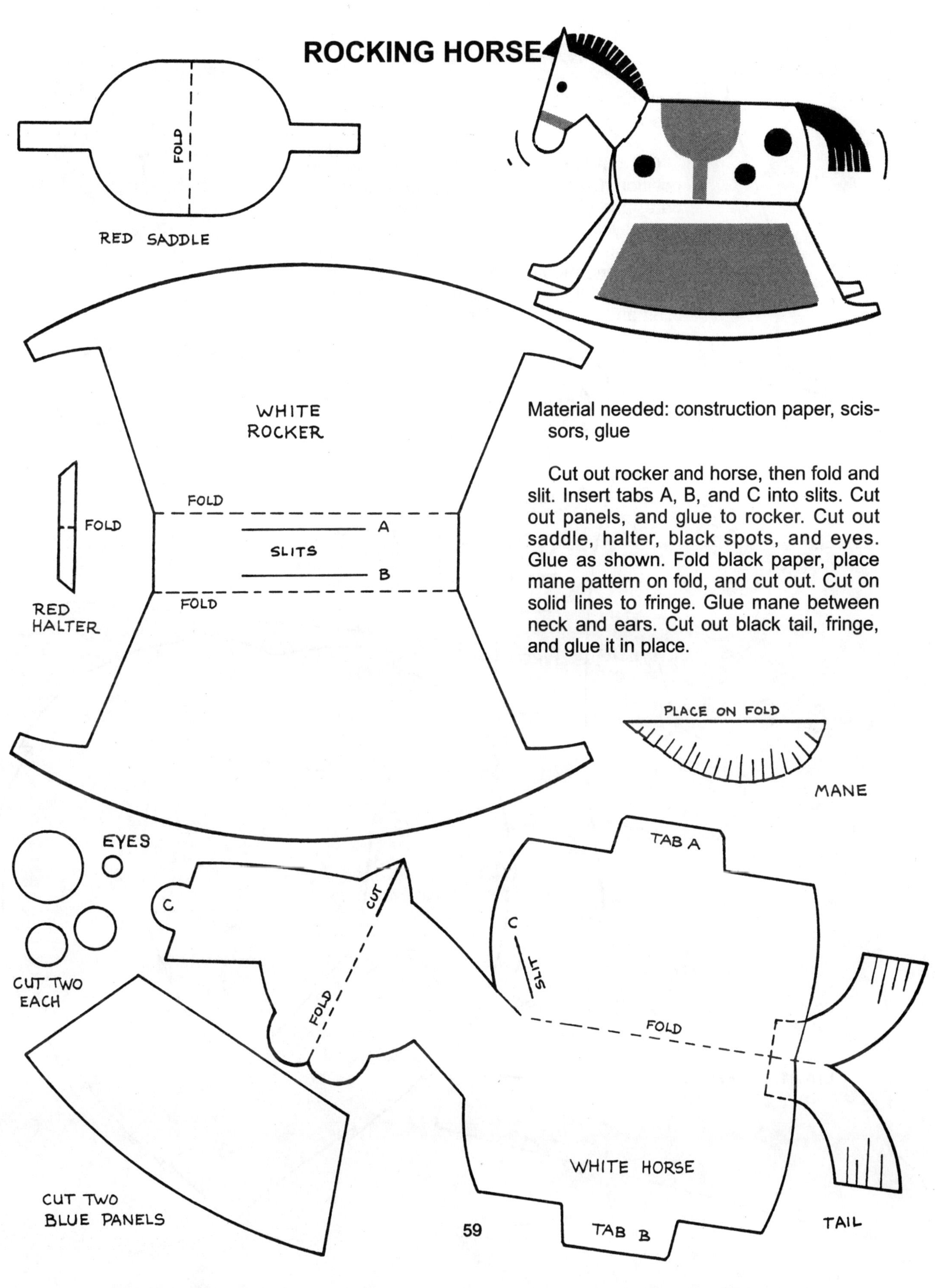

Material needed: construction paper, scissors, glue

Cut out rocker and horse, then fold and slit. Insert tabs A, B, and C into slits. Cut out panels, and glue to rocker. Cut out saddle, halter, black spots, and eyes. Glue as shown. Fold black paper, place mane pattern on fold, and cut out. Cut on solid lines to fringe. Glue mane between neck and ears. Cut out black tail, fringe, and glue it in place.

ROARING LION

Material needed: construction paper, scissors, glue

Cut out lion and front legs. Glue legs in position. Cut out lion's mane, nose, and two ears, and glue on. Cut slits in face. Cut out white eyelids and mouth. Cut out red tongue and glue on white mouth. Fold and insert eyelids and mouth into slits from the back of lion's head. Move from behind, making eyes blink and mouth open. Draw eyes.

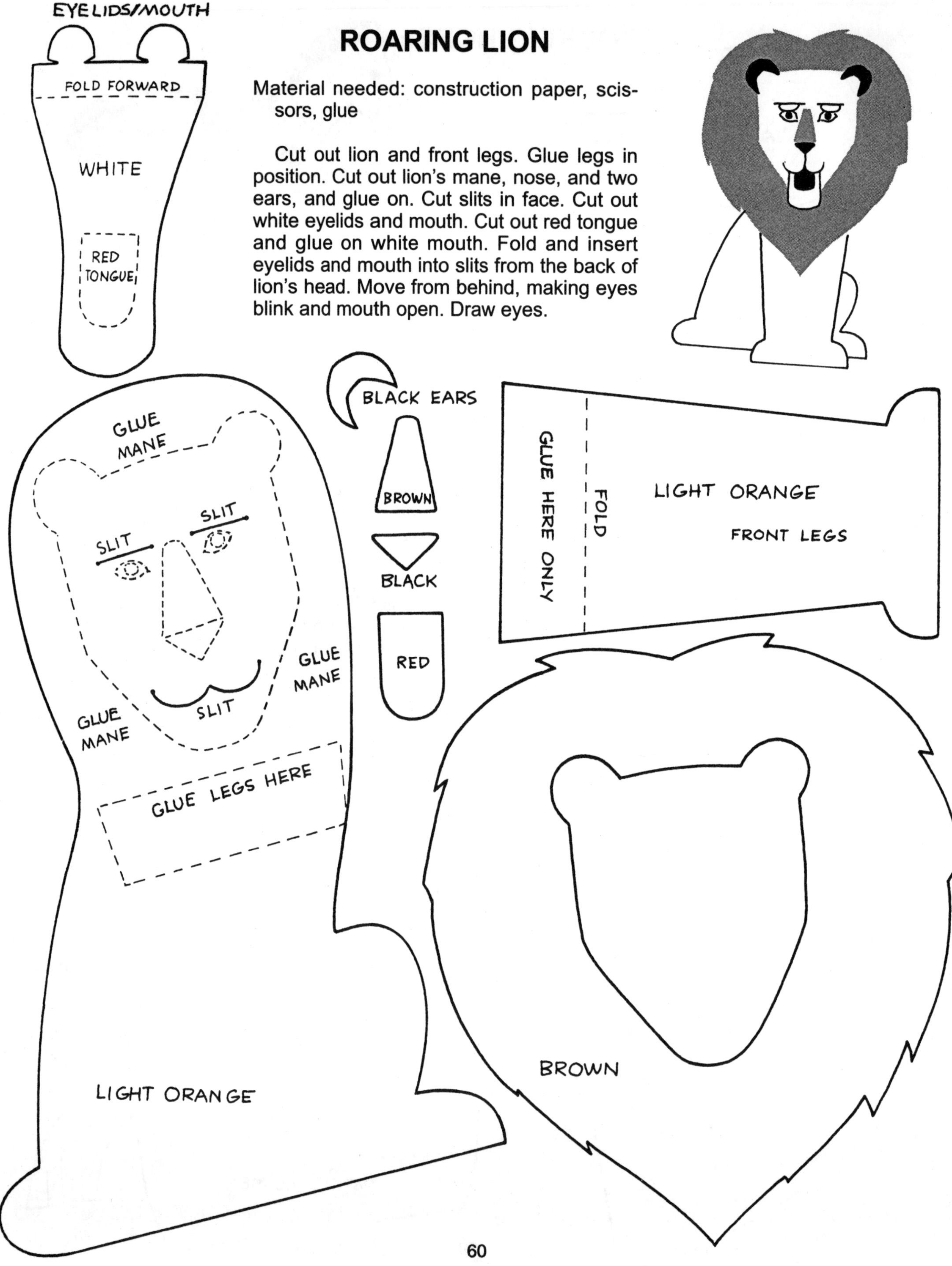

MERRY-GO-ROUND

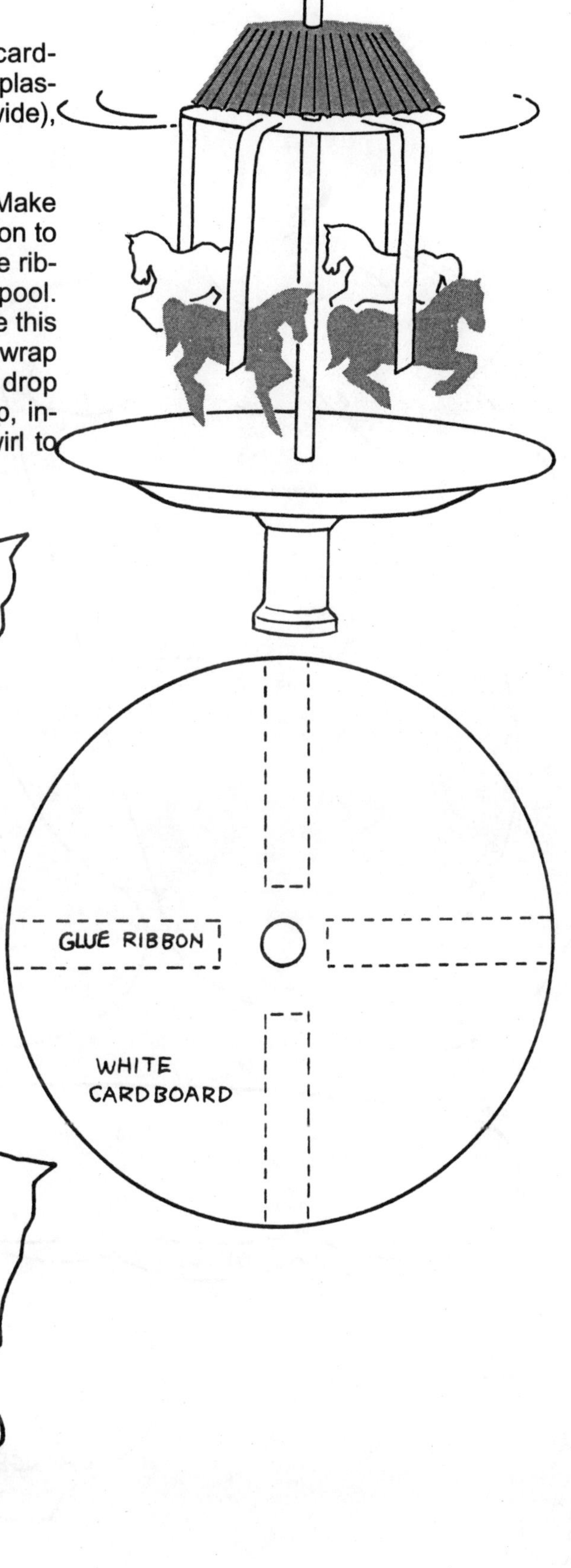

Material needed: construction paper, white cardboard, large spool, 7-inch paper plate, large plastic straw, four 4 3/4-inch ribbons (1/4 inch wide), paper cupcake cup, scissors, glue

Cut out white disk and two of each horse. Make a hole in center of disk. Glue one end of a ribbon to each horse as shown. Glue the other end of the ribbon to the disk. Put straw through hole in spool. Make a hole in the center of the plate, and slide this onto straw. About 2 inches from top of straw wrap cellophane tape around several times, then drop disk onto straw on top of tape. Add paper cup, inverted, with hole in center, onto the straw. Twirl to make the horses go round!

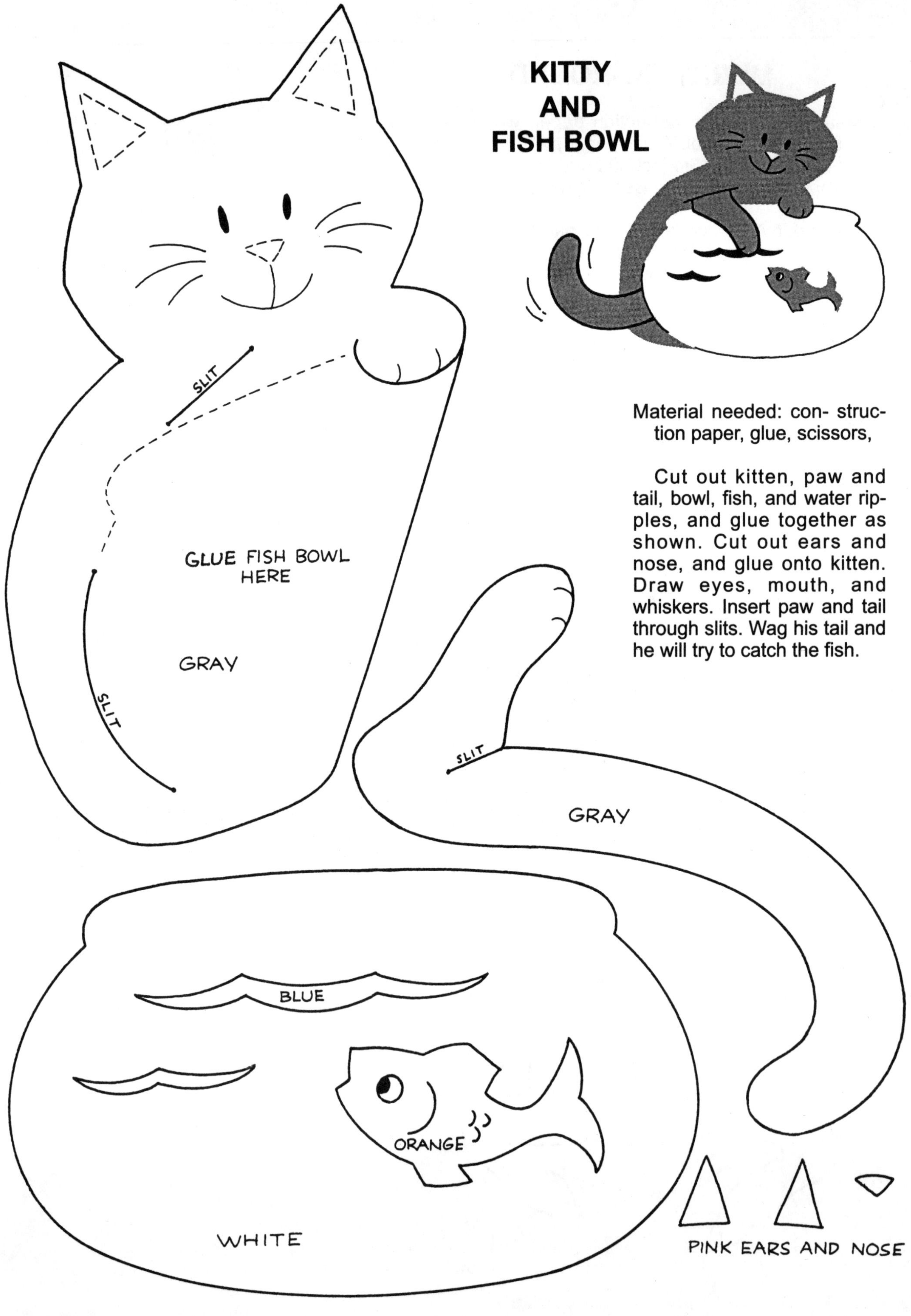

KITTY
AND
FISH BOWL
SLIT
GLUE FISH BOWL HERE
GRAY
SLIT
SLIT
GRAY
BLUE
ORANGE
WHITE
PINK EARS AND NOSE
Material needed: con- struc- tion paper, glue, scissors,
Cut out kitten, paw and tail, bowl, fish, and water rip- ples, and glue together as shown. Cut out ears and nose, and glue onto kitten. Draw eyes, mouth, and whiskers. Insert paw and tail through slits. Wag his tail and he will try to catch the fish.

WALKING DUCK

Material needed: construction paper, scissors, glue, paper fastener

Cut out two ducks. Cut out wheel and feet. Glue feet on both sides of wheel. Put wheel between ducks, and insert fastener at dots. Glue heads and tails of ducks together and cut slits. Cut out wings and insert through slits. Make duck walk by rolling forward on wheel. Finish by cutting out hat, trim, eyes, and bills. Glue these to both sides of duck.

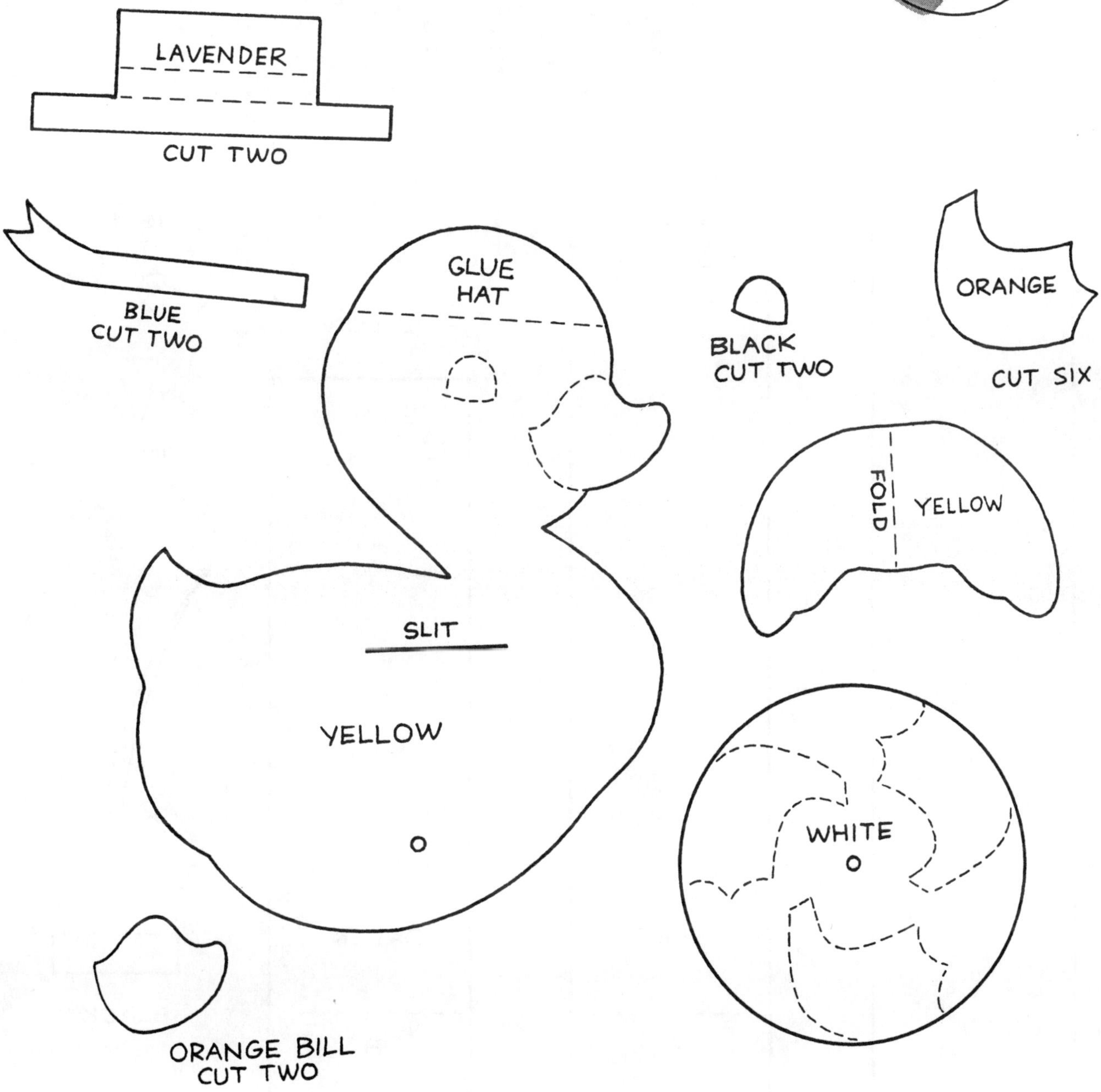

LAVENDER

CUT TWO

BLUE
CUT TWO

GLUE
HAT

BLACK
CUT TWO

ORANGE

CUT SIX

FOLD

YELLOW

SLIT

YELLOW

WHITE

ORANGE BILL
CUT TWO

CATERPILLAR

Material needed: construction paper, notebook reinforcements, scissors, glue

Cut out one C, one D, and 6 E's. C is the base, D is the head, the E's are the body. Glue A's to A's and B's to B's to form circles. Glue D and E's on base (Fig. 1). For the face, cut black patch and glue to yellow face. Glue two reinforcements on top of black for eyes. Cut out and glue red nose and two black feelers.